STEPHANIE BRUSH

LINDEN PRESS/SIMON & SCHUSTER

NEW YORK 1985

Men
An Owner's Manual

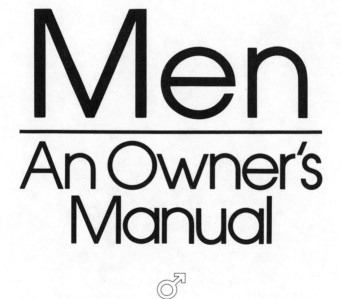

TO RICHARD

Copyright © 1984 by Stephanie Brush
All rights reserved
including the right of reproduction
in whole or in part in any form
Published by Linden Press/Simon & Schuster
A Division of Simon & Schuster, Inc.
Simon & Schuster Building
Rockefeller Center
1230 Avenue of the Americas
New York, New York 10020
LINDEN PRESS/SIMON & SCHUSTER and colophon are trademarks of
Simon & Schuster, Inc.
Designed by Karolina Harris
Manufactured in the United States of America
5 7 9 10 8 6
1 3 5 7 9 10 8 6 4 2 Pbk.
Library of Congress Cataloging in Publication Data
Brush, Stephanie.
Men : an owner's manual.
1. Men—Anecdotes, facetiae, satire, etc. I. Title.
PN6231.M45B7 1984   818'.5402   84-5687
ISBN 0-671-49459-7
ISBN 0-671-60413-9 Pbk.

CONTENTS

1. Man, The Concept   7

A History of Men   9
So Why Invest in a Man at All?   10
Structuring the Deal: Degrees of Living Together   13
How Do You Know If You Are Living With a Man?
   (Already)   15
Three Technicalities   17
How Do You Find a Man to Live With?   20
What to Avoid: A Cautionary Tale   22
Yearning for the High-Concept Man   24
Vintages of Men   27
Special Guide to Living with Foreign Men   30
Men: An Anthropological View   34

2. Man in the Home   45

NeatStyles   47
Bathrooms   52
Kitchen Details   55
The Vermin Issue   58
The Place of Wit in the American Home   60
Sleeping Together   62
The Sleeping-with-a-Man Film Festival   66
Pets   70
Special Occasions   73

3. Man in Practice 79

The Wielding of Power   81
Stupid Voices in Our Time   83
Oral Sex   84
Moments of Exquisite Crisis: Old Girlfriends   86
Old Boyfriends   89
His Mother   91
Your Mother   94
"Vengeance Is Mine," Sayeth the Lord. "Whether
    You Should Mess with It Is Another Story."   95
Advanced Arguing: Psychology in the Home   97
How to Fight About Money   99
Sexual Problems   102
Coping with His Infidelity   106
Closeness Exercises   108
How About "Couple Therapy"?   109
Role Models   112

4. Man Made Perfect 119

Dressing Your Man, From the Inside Out   121
A Little Off the Top: The Indignity of Hair Loss   125
The Care and Feeding of the Infirm Man   128
Dentistry and Your Man: The Cruel Truth   131
Getting Through to Men: The Incredible Sulk   133
The Stressed Man   137
Midlife Crisis   141
Getting Your Man Together and Taking Him on the
    Road   143

Epilogue: Some Parting Words to Live By 151

1. Do Not Think About Trying to Make It Through a
   Lifetime With a Man. Just Concentrate on Making
   It Through a Year.   154
2. Men Really Are Superior to Women in Many
   Ways   155
3. Men Want Love and Acceptance Just as Much
   as Women Do   156

1

Man,
The Concept

A HISTORY OF MEN

MEN have always been with us in one form or another. The study of *living* with men (or higher-animal husbandry) is fairly new.

There have been civilizations that have consisted entirely of women. (The educational film *Hercules and the Queen of the Amazons* shows us that these civilizations were made up mostly of women who talked much like Zsa Zsa Gabor; who had primitive facsimiles of push-up bras; and who said things like, *"My wanton heart is a flower panting to be pluck'd."* According to this and other films, Greco-Roman Amazon civilization could not have survived without extremely embarrassing dialogue, extremely embarrassing poetry, and push-up bras.)

Men were common in the Middle Ages: doing things with lances, sitting at round tables, rehearsing plainsongs in very high voices, and other activities. But men have been at their most attractive, throughout the ages, when they were not around. During World War II, women learned to "love a man in uniform" because he was a man who was going places—such as Omaha Beach, Iwo Jima, and Midway.

In the fifties, there were no men at all: They were either working at their advertising agencies, driving in their Chryslers, listening to Four Freshmen records, or locked in the bathroom discovering embarrassing body odor. No one ever had sex.

And then a great social revolution occurred, and men

ventured back into the public eye, because *everyone* was having sex (due to space-age contraceptives), and men wanted to be part of the action.

These were dynamic, fast-and-loose times: Women no longer spoke to men of outmoded issues like "morality." Men gorged themselves on an all-you-can-eat buffet of sensual opportunities—they were being invited to live (together, in the same house) with women, and no one felt the need to invest in color-coordinated hand towels. No one invested in much of anything: Men could say, "Listen honey, I'm going out tonight. For about a year, okay?" And women did not like this much.

Men drastically lost their popularity; women lost *their* popularity to a large degree, too; and everyone became completely confused.

SO WHY INVEST IN A MAN AT ALL?

THERE are still a number of very sound reasons, and don't listen to anybody who tells you there aren't.

Now that the eighties are upon us (and so far they've been a terrible idea—there's no denying that), we all have hard practical considerations to take into account. Among them, safety: Living completely alone can be terribly unwise. Self-defense manuals will tell you, "When living alone and answering the door, always yell, 'I'll get it, Bruce!' for the benefit of whatever pervert is lurking on the other side."

Well. I, for one, come from a long line of unconvincing liars. Lying in a low voice is one thing, but lying at extremely high decibel levels is outside the range of many women's capabilities. Life in the eighties is war. If a real Bruce will help you sleep nights, and he's making himself available, are you sure you want to fight him off?

Some women insist that pets, and even fine furniture, can fill the same function as men in one's life. Many women swear by cats. Actually, cats are much more difficult than men. Men do not give you small rodents as kiss-and-make-up gifts, men do not try to eat everything smaller than they are, and men do not require tiny little doors just to be let out of the house.

Many women insist that living with a man is a hindrance to getting to know one's "selfhood." But living with one's "selfhood" has become inconvenient for a number of reasons. It is difficult to share the rent with one's selfhood. It is difficult to fold sheets with one's selfhood. It is very silly to bring one's selfhood home to meet one's parents since, presumably, you've all already met.

But I won't kid you with a lot of cogent reasoning and fancy talk and intricately crafted arguments—

The Main Reason to Live with a Man:

You will never have to go on dates again. The principal difference between dates and Nazi torture is that Nazi torture took place in the 1940s and was seriously criticized at the Nuremburg trials. Dating, however, is STILL LEGAL and remains one of the least-understood atrocities that humans can commit. (Why, one wonders, is "to date" a transitive verb—something you do to another person? You could replace the verb "to date" with "to offend," "to assault," or "to dive-bomb.")

ANY NORMAL WOMAN OUT OF HIGH SCHOOL WHO DOES NOT WANT TO THROW UP BEFORE A DATE IS PROBABLY ON DRUGS, OR MENTALLY DEFICIENT. (For what it's worth, this is probably true of men, too.)

Casual dating (which is already a contradiction in terms) brings up so many irksome, niggling questions:

- Will you enjoy each other's company?
- Will you laugh at the same places in the movie?
- Will you agree, afterward, that you've *seen* the same movie?

- Will he want to pay for the meal?
- Will you need to pay him for paying for the meal?

If you are living with a man you do not have to worry about whether you should sleep with him after dinner. Which is to say, you'd bleeding well *better* sleep with him; but at least it's a black-and-white issue—there are no fine points of law involved. And if you are living with a man, he won't respect you any less in the morning than he does now.

A lot of women say, "I'm afraid to live with a man. He'll know *everything* about me."

Every women has an "It" about herself that she doesn't want known. Something private and dark and terrible. Lizzie Borden, for example, had a tough time on evenings out after she was acquitted, whenever her date said, "So, do your folks live in the area?" Once you begin living with a man, though, he forgives many of your trespasses, and you even forget rapidly what dates used to be like: God is merciful. (All you have to do is spend an evening with a single friend and *her* date to remember the horror of it all over again. Watch the anguish on your friend's face as her date mispronounces "Fassbinder" or makes Chinaman jokes or eats his salad with his oyster fork.)

Another Good Reason

Living with a man means, at least theoretically, not having to sit home and wait for him to call. You will look back with amazement on the days when you were expecting a call from some Special Guy. You canceled all your appointments for two days, filled a Hefty bag with Doritos, and camped out by the phone table. Sometimes you turned the phone upside down to see if all the wires were connected. When the phone rang, it was your mother, and you screamed into the receiver. Then you waited some more.

When darkness fell, you did not turn on the lights. You did not turn on the television or read a book, because your heart was pounding so fast that the excitement of reading *Martin Chuzzlewit* yet again would give you a coronary. You rehearsed the nonchalant tone you would affect when the call finally came.

Only it didn't.

Further Good Reasons

People often decide to live together simply because they need more personal contact in an impersonal world. Some claim this "contact" can be provided just as easily by one's immediate family, or even by another *woman*, but they are mistaken. Living with your family after the age of twenty-one is admitting that they have a Monopoly on your life. It is returning to "GO" without collecting two hundred dollars.

As for female roommates: They are indeed kind, loyal, thrifty, brave, and obedient; as well as modern and politically acceptable to other women. But all too often living with another woman is like waking up in the middle of a Rona Jaffe novel. Do you really want to spend the rest of your adult life arguing about who ate the last Figurine? Can another woman give you grandchildren?

And there can be no better reason for favoring men than this: esthetics. All male roommates at 7 A.M. look appreciably rumpled, yet adorable. They exude innocence, huggableness—a sort of helpless, charming *je ne sais quoi*.

All female roommates at 7 A.M. look like Lon Chaney.

No one knows why this is true, but it is.

STRUCTURING THE DEAL: DEGREES OF LIVING TOGETHER

THE options available to you, when you take on a man these days, can be bewildering. Should you take him on an open-ended, strictly tryout basis, or should you go for the whole enchilada and make him legally Yours? ("For better or for worse . . . 'til death do you part," which is roughly equivalent to a lifetime warranty, although loopholes in this arrangement seem to surface every day.)

Taking on a man "for the time being" is a popular, low-risk policy. It tends to make some women "insecure." (Although there is an ongoing argument about whether marriage makes women more or less "insecure." The popular witticism "Take my wife . . . please" has caused consternation in many married women, as it implies that men's faith in the institution is, at best, incomplete.)

Marriage in the eighties has a more modern, youthful, streamlined feel than it's had in past decades; and it is surely much more of a free-enterprise endeavor than it is in many *foreign* countries. (In some countries, your parents decide before you are five years old who you should spend the rest of your life with, and you do not question their judgment. They have, after all, consulted tarot cards and astrologers, and traded several camels and bales of cloth, and a few eggplants, in your behalf. Marriage is a big, cold business. No one really cares if you and your intended like the same rock bands.)

Marriage makes many feel that they have truly reached adulthood. Try it, and you suddenly become important enough in your community to warrant several columns of newsprint, and soon the whole world knows you have been "betrothed" or "affianced." (Although no one knows how to pronounce these words since no one has ever used them in a conversation.)

However, you should not spend too much time involving yourself in technicalities, since men are men and come with the same standard options, whether you choose to own, borrow, or rent.

HOW DO YOU KNOW IF YOU ARE LIVING WITH A MAN? (ALREADY)

YOU used to know you were living with a man if
- You had been carried over a threshold, wearing something in white peau de soie;
- You read *Bride's, Bride, Today's Bride,* and *Modern Bride* and you were comfortable referring to knives and forks as "flatware";
- You were having regular sex and no one had to get up and go home afterward.

Don't look for this kind of clarity in modern life. It isn't there. As we have seen, nowadays, the only difference between marrieds and unmarrieds is that married people have a signed legal document, and better dishes.

The complications come in when you are somewhere in between. Unfortunately, ALTHOUGH YOU CANNOT BE SORT OF PREGNANT OR SORT OF MARRIED OR SORT OF DEAD-ON-ARRIVAL, YOU CAN BE "SORT OF LIVING WITH SOME-ONE."

Let's say you're at a restaurant with a friend one day. (Although living with a man means "forsaking all others," you do occasionally "lunch with others.")

"Hey," your friend says in a having-been-forsaken sort of voice. "We hardly ever *see* you anymore."

"Well," you will say (and you will just sort of realize it *as you are saying it*), "I'm sort of living with somebody."

You had probably been getting some warning signs along the way:
- You were screening his mail from Publishers' Clearing House.
- You were taking regular phone calls from his mother, and she wasn't just saying, "Hello, is Petey there?"

- You were already going to the Safeway together, and buying *twelve eggs,* not ripping the boxes in half.
- You find yourself constantly accepting invitations in the "we," even though you are not a nurse or the Queen of England.
- You have worn his underwear. Without shame.

Unfortunately, even this manual cannot tell you whether you are *definitely* living with a man. It can only hand you probabilities. There are many reasons for this. Many men have nightmares that women will take advantage of the gray areas in today's social rules—that a woman will move in slowly, inexorably, bobby pin by bobby pin, so that by the time the man realizes what she's up to it will actually take legal action to eject her.

Some couples try to avoid this unwholesome process by announcing, "Okay, okay, let's live together," meaning that they have to set a date (although the only "guests" that will show up will be a couple of guys with a truck).

Other couples try to force the issue by breaking up entirely. (Known as "breaking up, but not *really* breaking up.") They have a terrible argument, avow that they never want to see each other again, and tell all their friends that they never want to see each other again. Then they wait forty-eight hours and move in together. (This crisis is always solved in the movies by getting married immediately.)

You have to understand that men can be awfully sluggish about making decisions of the heart. Remember, please, that evolution is a slow process. Amphibians didn't exactly *decide* to become reptiles. One day, one brave, scaly green guy took a long walk on land and cautiously said, "Okay, okay, I can handle this." That's how life science is.

THREE TECHNICALITIES

1. Your Place or His?

Originally you had a house and he had a house. Living together *really* begins when you give up one of these domiciles permanently, which sounds pretty scary, but the Flying Wallendas do all kinds of things without a safety net, and you don't hear them complaining, do you?

There is great advantage to your moving all your things at great angst, expense, and aggravation. YOU CAN HOLD IT AGAINST HIM FOR THE REST OF YOUR LIFE TOGETHER. The next time he tells you you're unbearable, you can say

- "I gave up RACQUETBALL ON THE PREMISES FOR YOU."
- "I gave up TWENTY-FOUR-HOUR SECURITY AND UNDERGROUND PARKING FOR YOU."
- "I gave up ACORN SQUASH (or other appropriate home-garden products) FOR YOU."

Of course, if you move into his place, you will be surrounded by many items you will at first not understand the significance of: his Lava lamp, his stuffed whale, his shower curtain, which is beyond filth but, rather resembles something they'd wrap the bodies in after an insurgence at a Turkish prison.

But hang in there—women are intrinsically more *flexible* than men, and you should use this to your advantage more often.

2. Lease Legality

Unfortunately, despite the words of the old song, the law does not recognize that "anywhere you hang your hat is home." The law has seen too many hats in too many unsuitable locales, and the law is sick and tired of these shenanigans. If you are not married to your man, you cannot tell his landlord that you are using his place simply as a *pied-à-terre*. The landlord will think that a *pied-à-terre* is some kind of cockamamie French casserole, and he will not thank you for mocking his erudition.

Cohabitation laws vary from state to state, but most states are clearly in favor of "members of his immediate family." The law would actually look the other way if he were to cohabit with his possessive mother, or his strumpet sister, or his disturbed brother with the termite collection, who writes pornographic letters to Olivia Newton-John.

If your guy's landlord tries to evict you without just cause, bear in mind that you are dealing with a form of intelligence that rivals pond life in sheer baseness. Do not go to court about this. Do not settle out of court. Settle out of town. Permanently.

3. What Do You Call the Man You Live With? Besides Al.

Semantics never used to rear their ugly heads in one's personal life. Somehow there used to be a lot more useful words floating around when it came to affairs of the heart. You had words that were both more and less specific than "relationship," and both more and less tiresome. You had "liaison." You had "ménage" (above a certain income level you had it, anyway). You had (and have), if you are lucky in this area, "marriage."

The person to whom you are *not* married, with whom you are living, has continued to defy easy description in polite society.

- "This is my guy," you say, and you feel like one of Martha and the Vandellas.
- "This is my old man," you say, and you feel like Grace Slick. Grace Slick twenty years ago.
- "This is my boyfriend," you say, and you feel seventeen. Everyone at the black-tie dinner thinks your parents are still waiting up for you in Fair Lawn, New Jersey.

- "This is my POSSLQ," you say, and you sound like a federal agent. (POSSLQ—for Persons of Opposite Sex Sharing Living Quarters—is also the name of an Amazonian rodent, and the two usages are often confused, with often-tragic results.)
- "This is my *roomie*," you say, and you feel like part of a midseason replacement sitcom on CBS.

You could not introduce him.

You could never refer to him at all in the third person. This involves waving your left arm a lot and uttering incomplete sentences. As in, "Last weekend I went to the beach house with ah-h-h-h-h . . ."

The term "live-in" has been coined by some, and not just to describe the upstairs maid. (Some people like to get together in small packs and viciously transmute perfectly harmless, respectable verbs without regard for the standards, or the welfare, of society. Many of these people work for popular magazines and are outside the law.) I might point out, additionally, that no one ever says "*my* live-in," but rather "*his* live-in," or "*her* live-in."

If you have the élan to carry it off, it is really nifty to grab your guy by the small of his waist and say to your friends, "May I have your attention, please? This is my *lover*, Xavier." (It helps if your lover is actually *named* something like "Xavier," but this is all too rarely the case.) Your relatives will hate it, but your *friends* will go crazy.

At least when you are talking to your parents, you should try to instill good habits in them by always referring to your guy by his Christian name. (Even if he isn't Christian. Even if he isn't *Judeo*-Christian.) It will take your mother approximately two and a half years to learn the name of the guy you're living with. (She's doing it to hurt you. Just so you know.)

If you're able to take the long view about it, it doesn't really matter what you call the guy you live with. American Language Scientists are working around the clock to find a cure for this strange deficiency in American usage. Have faith in them. When they make their breakthrough, you will hear about it in time.

In *Time*.

HOW DO YOU FIND A MAN TO LIVE WITH?

YOU should shop for men, the way you shop for shoes or puppies or tomatoes. And it's not easy—you can't tell all the important things about a man just by sniffing him or squeezing him or walking him around the block.

How do you know what his past record is like? Is he secretly married? If he isn't married, what's wrong with him? Pay careful attention to his manners. The most important quality to look for in a man is CONSIDERATION.

- Does he pay attention to you when you want him to pay attention to you?
- Does he leave you alone when you want to be left alone?
- Does he pay attention to you when you say you want to be left alone but actually you're just *saying* you want to be left alone, so that he'll pay attention to you?

Here are some commonly asked questions about the problem of finding a man:

Q. How can I meet a man who's—you know—*right* for me?

A. Meeting a man through mutual friends is still the most popular means. It's clean, it's safe, it's American, and you get to do it in relative privacy. Also, you have set up a chain of accountability—just as there was in the U.S. Defense Department in the 1960s. If anything goes wrong, you know exactly whom never to speak to again, whose house to napalm—whatever.

Q. How will this "meeting" take place?

A. If you tell your friends you are available, they will very likely set you up on something called a "blind date," which is sort of like a *real* date, except that instead of wanting to throw up beforehand, you usually want to throw up *during*.

Q. Should I live with a man I've just met by chance? How do I really know if he's on the up-and-up?

A. How does he know *you're* on the up-and-up? He doesn't know where *you've* been either. Taking chances is what life is all about. It's always Russian roulette. You can't *really* tell in the dim, stale light of a bar 'n' grill whether his teeth are real, whether his wallet leather is real, and whether's he's ever had a disease that's been on the cover of *Time* magazine.

If you're really worried about the guy, test-drive him by one of your close friends and see what *she* says. Life is very cruel and often provokes us into physical attractions with subnormal, maladjusted, or otherwise-unacceptable persons. Even pathological criminals often walk around with clean hankies, manicured fingernails, and fresh pennies in their loafers.

Q. Should I look for a man with lots of money?

A. Let's put it this way: You can't have sex with money. It would look very odd. What you get, after all is said and done, is the man *himself,* and even very wealthy men take off their pants one leg at a time (although no woman has ever been able to figure out what this expression means). According to surveys, most women cite "love" as the best reason for living with a man. ("A pathological clawing need for security" is a close second, but "love" is still very popular.)

How you react to the presence of tangible wealth says a lot about your character. There are those who have said, "The Mercedes is the Rorschach test of the modern age." Many women have fantasies that a man in a Mercedes will drive up to them and say, "Wow, Mavis, I haven't seen you since high school!"

Ultimately, though, the coveting of trinkets leads to a life of surface glamour and shallow ideals.

Q. How can I tell the difference between a good life and a life of surface glamour and shallow ideals; and how can I attain the latter?

A. If you have a name like Mavis, you have no business aspiring to the latter.

Q. How important is a sense of humor in a man?

A. It is true that some men eschew whimsy in the home. (They are known as Whimsy Eschewers, and I do not recommend their cultivation.) They are very often U.S. government scientists, fire-prevention experts, and NASA mission specialists, and are men who, to put it bluntly, are not likely to let a smile be their umbrella.

But we need men like these to oil the wheels of society.

We need all kinds of men to oil the wheels of society. We need men, period. The best I can say to you is caveat emptor. Keep your eyes open, and keep his name off your checks until you're *really* sure about him.

WHAT TO AVOID: A CAUTIONARY TALE

THERE are men among us who expect *everything to go their way*.

These men were exceedingly close to their mothers, and their mothers protected them from life's more appalling rigors: They were never forced to view violence or poverty. They never knew that laundry, when soiled, had to be rendered *un*soiled by some luckless human or other. They had really keen birthday parties, with ponies, every year.

Such a man's mother could actually tell, at birth, that no female human *would ever be good enough for him*. She alone could see the little corona that surrounded his head at birth, signifying that *this* boy was

An American Prince.

When the American Prince reaches adulthood, he faces a rude awakening. (He *faces* this awakening, note. I never said that he actually awakens.) This man demands a lot out of life. He *expects* stoplights never to be red. He expects all car washes to be sixty second. He expects elevators not to stop at floors *where he doesn't want to go.*

And men like this always seem to end up with rather hapless sorts of women. Women for whom *nothing* ever goes quite right. And maybe you're one of them. You got strep throat on the night you were supposed to play the Queen of the Pond Fairies in the school play. You got potentially fatal cramps on prom night. Your mother made you get a monumentally gross haircut the summer you turned thirteen, and you had to spend the entire months of July and August in the house, only going out after dark or in disguise. Your car stalls regularly in the Exact Change lane at tollbooths, and your relatives misspell your name on greeting cards.

And something about a very Princely guy seems to attract you. Okay, okay, he complains a lot; and some uncharitable people even use the word *obnoxious* to describe this man. . . . But you have noticed in your brief, sometimes-tragic life span that a guy who complains a lot is *a guy who gets things done.* (As he has most assuredly told you.)

Living with him, your doors never squeak. Your faucets never drip. Your TV picture is always like the one in magazines that's labeled "a simulation."

But be warned—a Princely, Complaining Man will invariably embarrass you in public. He will take you to Arby's and say, "Waiter, I specifically ordered this roast beef on the *pink* side," and ask to see the manager. IT IS THE BIRTHRIGHT OF THE AMERICAN PRINCE TO "ASK TO SEE THE MANAGER" WHENEVER *ANYTHING* GOES CONTRARY TO HIS NEEDS.

American Princes have been known to "ask to see managers"
- at the zoo;
- on white-water rafting trips;
- at lemonade stands;
- on bumper-car rides;
- in church.

Whenever the Prince humiliates you in public, you can always try the time-honored approach of acting as if you've never met him before, but sooner or later he'll wave in your direction and say, "And I'm sure Peggy here is *very* upset about what's being done to us," and then everyone will stare at you with a mixture of pity and loathing; and you'll wish that you could just Disappear into the Asphalt.

If you can avoid getting sucked into this man's orbit, your life on this planet will turn out immeasurably better. Don't stand there like a little idiot, babbling that "love is blind."

Wear your *glasses,* for Pete's sake.

YEARNING FOR THE HIGH-CONCEPT MAN

MOST women have very active fantasy lives, and most of our fantasies revolve around HIGH-CONCEPT MEN.

A high-concept man is one you can describe to your friends in less than three words: ZAP, ZAP, ZAP. Our friends get an instant image of what kind of guy he is.

When you were fifteen, the following were high-concept men: "Monkee." "Biker." "Rhythm guitarist." "Lifeguard." Our limbic system responded to them at a very primitive level. We would let them take us under an amusement pier, or driving out past the New Lots, or into their living rooms when their parents were out of town.

These men still capture our imagination, because *we don't have to know anything about them* to know they turn us on. And now they come in new models—some of us can get completely lost in our fantasy lives if we're not careful. It's time to debunk some of these adult male versions of the H.C.M., because you may just never get around to doing it yourself.

Commercial Pilots

You want to know a guy with reflexes and motor skills like this. The possibilities involved in a high degree of hand-eye coordination cannot be overlooked.

But do you want to know a guy with ABSOLUTELY NO SENSE OF HUMOR? Commercial airlines do not take a chance on hiring humorous people. There is always a one-in-one-hundred-thousand chance that they will start doing Ed Sullivan imitations during takeoff.

Have you ever met a commercial pilot who said anything really funny? He thinks in a dull monotone even during sex. There's a little voice box in his head saying, ". . . and our estimated *(unintelligible)* of climax will be 1 A.M., Eastern Daylight Time *(unintelligible)* . . . ve a pleasant flight."

Heart Surgeons

A surgeon is as close as a man can get to being God. A *heart* surgeon doesn't even deign to be interested in being God. It would involve a cut in pay.

All heart surgeons (like all commercial pilots) come from Texas (or Arizona); and like commercial pilots they all have acutely good eyesight, subtly graying hair, and extremely well-shaped jawlines. They are all named Steve or Harold.

But heart surgeons usually have very little time for you. They would rather sit in hospital cafeterias and look at color centerfolds of naked aortic valves. What makes you think you could compete?

Cowboys

The guys who ride the horses in all those cigarette ads actually work for the Zoli modeling agency in New York City. They are all actually Dutch or Hungarian. You couldn't pronounce their names even if you wanted to.

Famous Writers

Somewhere the myth began that writers are sensitive people. No one knows why this is thought to be the case.

Writers undeniably know a lot of *words,* and they are capable of saying things like, "I admire your warmth, on a variety of levels"; but this should not be mistaken for actual *talking.* This is just a sentence. From anyone but a writer, it would be horribly embarrassing.

When writers argue with you, they say things like, "In a strictly Keynesian sense, I think *not,* Felicia," which makes you feel like about two cents. Writers are always smoking and smiling at something you don't understand, and you're never quite sure whether they're in the throes of Being Intelligent, and therefore not to be disturbed (because you'll risk being bored with the story of how Coleridge got interrupted while writing "Kubla Khan," and for the rest of his life never remembered the ending he had planned for it).

Additionally, everyone knows that novelists and poets never wash their hair.

U.S. Senators

John F. Kennedy popularized the notion that politicians should also be Hot Studs as well as statesmen. Nowadays, any politician with a modicum of animal magnetism is described as "Kennedyesque." In Sidney Sheldon novels, for example, U.S. senators are invariably spectacularly athletic lovers—and "Kennedyesque."

But politicians' stars have waned recently, for two reasons: It is unpopular nowadays for women to fantasize about being first ladies—the power *behind* the throne—where all you get to do is curtsy, wear tasteful Galanos dinner dresses, and nod meaningfully during the oath of office.

Secondly, elected officials have become Boobs of Record much too often in recent news. During the ABSCAM trials, we saw far too many of them on videotape taking money from FBI agents who were obviously wearing acrylic mustaches.

Nowadays, the only women who have legitimate fantasies about U.S. senators are stenographers and exotic dancers in Georgetown.

Firemen

All women want to grow up to marry firemen. Firemen aren't afraid of danger. They're strong. They're tall and handsome. They've got great lungs. Firemen are all named Dick or Hank, and they were not born of human parents.

Firemen call you "Miss." (A formality even gynecologists have dispensed with in these dissolute times.) They are frequently very shy. They carry long hoses. Firemen never yell at their Dalmations.

The moral of all this is unclear. Maybe if you're lucky you'll actually find yourself a fireman to live with, because I can't think of a single thing wrong with them. Sorry.

VINTAGES OF MEN

MEN who came of age in different eras are *very different products,* with different outlooks on life and personal prejudices. Different philosophies and experiences. Different blood pressure levels, hairlines, and of course record collections.

Naturally, it is quite insane to categorize *all* men simply by age in a page's worth of text.

But we can always give it a try, hey?

The Seventies Generation (Ages 20–29)

Men of the seventies are state-of-the-art male specimens. Nothing bad has ever happened in their lifetimes. Mention the Bay of Pigs invasion to them and they say, "Hey, is this going to be on the test?"

Men of the seventies are terrifyingly young. The Beatles have children their age. They do not remember a world without electric pianos or egg substitutes.

They have a lot of natural, untutored respect for women. They have more respect for women than *you* do. It can become revolting at times.

Men of the seventies, for example, believe in women's rights to form rock bands where they (women) sing and play *all the instruments*. (Not that these women are much to look at, mind you. No one with an eraser haircut and a fist ta-tooed on her nipple need be considered a serious threat to your future together. But they *call* themselves ominous things. The Waitresses. The Nymphos. The Sex Goblins. Their mothers certainly cannot know they are calling themselves this.) I feel that men's hearing of their music on the radio airwaves should be sharply curtailed.

They squeak far too attractively.

Men of the Sixties (Ages 30–39)

Literally millions of men reached the full flush of manhood in the sixties, although whether they reached maturity is another issue. Many men of the sixties are among us today —dating, marrying, recreating, procreating. (If you looked at their chromosomes under a microscope, they would re-semble alphabet soup from Venus; but we try not to ponder these things.)

Men of the sixties are mostly "straightened out" by now, but they feel cheated that they did not start their adult lives with the real tools of adulthood—they never learned to want a "real" job, never learned to stop beginning sentences with "Like . . . ," never learned to lie on a résumé. They are nostalgic in many ways for their past. They could never bring themselves to dispose of that last pair of buffalo sandals, that last Tom Paxton album with the candle drippings on the sleeve, that last pair of Maharishi Mahesh Yogi cotton drawstring pants.

Men of the sixties had a rude awakening at a crucial point in their lives: When the counterculture decamped, it seemed to disappear *overnight*. (Although it still survives in parts of Washington and Oregon, where there are still humans named "Bay Leaf," "Sun Ray," and "Compost" living in toolsheds.) For this reason, you should avoid living with your sixties man in either of these states.

Men of the Fifties (Ages 40 and Up)

These men feel the hot sting of injustice, because for most of their adult lives they were allowed to undress women with their eyes but seldom with any other part of their bodies. They may have suffered some glandular damage from this particular social stricture; but this is not always readily visible.

These men learned most of what they know about life from Holden Caulfield, Edward R. Murrow, and the Big Bopper. They tend to have rather unrealistic images of women, because deep down they are Afraid of Being Close. (They learned this in the fifties, when dancing close to a woman's hair meant risking facial lacerations.)

More than anything else, men of the fifties are terrorized by the idea of Phil Donahue. Here's a grown man with snow-white hair being paid to be real, immediate, and achingly vulnerable in public; to say each day to a roomful of perfectly strange women, *"Help me out* here. . . ."

Faced with this vision, men of the fifties always flip the dial, hoping Woody Woodpecker is on another channel.

SPECIAL GUIDE TO LIVING WITH FOREIGN MEN

IT is almost never advisable to live with a foreign man.

It's okay to be divorced from one or to have an affair or a sizzling correspondence with one. But if you decide to *live* with one, in the same country, you miss getting all those great stamps, and I must warn you that *les règles du jeu* change completely.

Still, you're not going to listen. If you are already sopping with passion over Oskar Werner or Jean-Louis Trintignant or another thin-lipped roué of their sort, only God can save you now.

Bear this in mind, though. Think of the future. WHAT IF YOU HAVE CHILDREN? They will be BILINGUAL children. They will be able to speak Swedish, or whatever it is, BETTER THAN YOU DO. Your children will be able to stand right in front of you, call you a monkey's snot ball, and you won't even know it.

But I see you're still not impressed. So on to the hard stuff.

Living with an English Man

They are undoubtedly the best. At least you don't have to learn suspicious conjugations just to *talk* to them.

And they can be taken anywhere. You can show up with them at Elaine's without a reservation, and someone will think they're Lord Snowdon and you'll get a great table.

You can take them to parties; they can get roaring drunk,
- call everyone in the room a bleeding sot,
- try to blow up balloons by sticking them up their nose, and

We so seldom take time to understand the habits of Easterners, and this is tragic.

Living with a South American Man

South American men do not try to kiss you on the first date. They reserve the first date for trying to marry you. Only the worst kind of tramp lives with a South American without being married.

When a South American man tells you you are wonderful, you rate very high indeed—right behind his mother, the Virgin Mary, and himself. South American men are very attractive. Brazilian men, for example, look better in bikinis than women do. That is why Rio de Janeiro is a beach, not a city. South American men like to have a good time. They like to dance, swim, and listen to music. If you are very nice, they will tell you about it afterward.

Living with an Eastern European Man

If you can fall in love with a man named Zdravko, you are probably beyond counsel. But you can be assured by this: Life with an E.E.M. is always an adventure. Sometimes he gets crazy and violent and unpleasantly picturesque, but he's never boring.

Czechs and Poles and Hungarians and the like are powerfully fond of telling their "I made it out alive" stories for all your friends. The stories get better every time: They had a chicken and a balalaika strapped to their waist, it was thirty degrees below zero, and they'd just had their ear shot off, but somehow by the light of morning, they managed to crawl into Austria.

There are drawbacks to E.E.M.s. Don't ever expect to tell them about *your* miserable childhood and get any sympathy. They'll get drunk, spit on you, and grind a cocktail glass into your heel. It's nothing personal.

MEN: AN ANTHROPOLOGICAL VIEW

EVEN though we have seen that cultural differences can create special ennuis in your dealings with men, there are some characteristics that men of all cultures share. Scientists called ANTHROPOLOGISTS have studied these traits, and they have been able to answer some of the most common questions women ask about men.

Why Are Women Smaller than Men?

Five million years ago, women were the same size as men, and they could run just as fast and jump just as high as men could. This meant that when men chased women, as their primitive cerebral impulses instructed them to do, the women always got away.

The human race died out six or seven times before anyone figured out that they had the whole formula wrong, and women started helpfully tripping over small pieces of brush, thereby getting pregnant and bringing Homo sapiens to the place where he is today. Somehow getting smaller inevitably followed.

The first man who could walk erect was very proud of himself. He walked around erect all the time, and women just sat and watched him walk around erect, and the human race died out three or four times before anyone figured out that lying down erect was probably a much better idea.

The theory of Creationism was set down by the (male) writers of the Bible as a sort of cover-up, because they didn't want anyone knowing that humans had blown it time and time again on such a massive scale.

Why Don't Men Carry Purses?

In prehistoric times, a man had to have his hands free to fight off predators and guys with bigger spears. For this reason, women became carriers. They always had a lot of STUFF in their hands. And to this day, men do not like to have STUFF in their hands; but if a woman leaves the house without carrying something, she feels mysteriously naked.

An evening purse is a vestige of the prehistoric age. A woman cannot fit anything useful in an evening purse, but at least it's something to carry.

What men have instead of hands is pockets. The average man's suit jacket contains anywhere from two to 380 pockets, including the invisible ones that no woman ever knows about. In these pockets a man can carry: His keys. Fight tickets. Combs and nail-grooming accessories. Spare Kleenex, for when you start to cry uncontrollably in the car for no reason. Spanish-English dictionary. Pens. Flashlight. Address and appointment books. Five-year calendars. Money. Checkbook. Credit cards. Pictures of cousins. Good-luck charms. Bottle opener. Memo pads. Airplane tickets. Dental floss. Passports. None of these items ever bulge.

He cannot understand why you need to carry a purse, or what you put in it. But he still has his hands free to fight off predatory animals and guys with bigger spears.

Why Are Men Always Fixing Things That Aren't Broken, and Ruining Them?

Let us say you are home one evening enjoying a spate of relaxing television, oblivious to the outside world, when your man saunters into the room and stops dead in his tracks.

"That picture is terrible," he says.

"Why is it terrible?" you say.

"The Mandrell Sisters are green," he says.

"They look fine," you say. *"Don't touch it."*

(You could say anything you want at this point, because the situation is already completely out of control. He is going to fiddle with the knobs for the next half-hour, and forget whatever it is you are watching.)

This is known as the *Mega-fix*. It is the phenomenon whereby a man takes something marginally not in working order and renders it into working *dis*order. Vacuum cleaners are prime candidates for this. The modern man can take a vacuum with a vague hiccup and infect it with a fascinating electronic version of the whooping cough—and in just under twenty minutes, too.

Men do not like to fix things that are broken. They like to "improve" things that are not broken.

Why do men do this? Probably when they were little, they saw Dad going down into the basement with the power tools, and they realized that Dad was forging a means of symbolic separation from Mom. Mom knew better than to bring up touchy subjects when Dad was reaming out a hunk of pine with a look of ferocious glee in his eye. If she wanted to talk, she'd have to scream, and then he'd be well within his rights when he said, "Marie, why the hell are you *screaming* at me?"

In addition to answering these perplexing questions, anthropologists have isolated four IMPERATIVES which seem to typify men of all cultures, races, and levels of development.

IN ORDER TO LIVE EFFECTIVELY WITH A MAN, YOU MUST UNDERSTAND THESE FOUR IMPERATIVES. Otherwise you are up a creek without oarlocks.

We are going to examine these four imperatives in depth.

1. The Toy Imperative

Until the day when you actually find your man in bed with his Sansui TU-S77AMX digital synthesis AM/FM tuner, you probably have nothing serious to worry about.

But you should know that all grown men believe passionately in the World of Toys—in consoles, in things that go click and "ping," in rows of colored lights, in dimmer switches; in anything that comes in a box labeled "batteries not included." ("C'*mon*, honey," men say breathlessly, their cheeks flushed, their temples moist, "let's go out to K Mart for *batteries!*") They never particularly notice the degree to which you do not share in their enthusiasm.

Why don't women grow up loving toys in the same way men do?

Let's take a look at some of the toys little girls play with. Let's take Barbie, for example. Girls want to grow up to *be* Barbie. That's the whole point of the exercise. Girls want to meet a Ken and buy a dream house and wear nifty outfits— girls want to *become* the toys they play with. And when they grow up, they're too busy worrying about whether Ken will voice a preference for Stove Top stuffing over potatoes to get nostalgic about youth anymore: Adult Reality is much too arduous.

But a boy does not become a train. He does not *become* Vac-U-Form, or an ant farm. Thus, at age twenty-one, a man's best Toy Years are still ahead of him. Inwardly he never wants to stop sending away for the prizes on cereal boxes.

Men remain very emotional about their toys. The same man who can discuss sexual dysfunction and midlife crisis with admirable stoicism will become extremely emotional about premature Clogged Heads on his VCR. (Men can be easily disillusioned about lapses in Toy Technology. The worst moment in a man's young life was the moment he discovered that Alvin and the Chipmunks were just a bunch of guys singing with their voices speeded up.)

Let's say that your man has just purchased a stereo system where the price of each individual speaker could feed the population of Taiwan

- and there's a "thump" in one of the speakers;
- and he's been making furtive, hushed calls to "Jimmy in the Service Department";
- and he wants to name your first child after "Jimmy in the Service Department";
- and you say that you are not going to name your first child after a guy with a tattoo that says, "I ♡ TWEETERS."

He will feel that you are being disloyal and uncooperative.

A man slaves over his toys with a SINGLE-MINDEDNESS that he feels women would do well to emulate. If he just spent the last five weekends in his garage adjusting the rising-rate rear suspension on his Yamaha XJ900, he needs to be reminded that eating, sleeping, and eliminating are occasionally necessary to the sustenance of human life.

(Be wary of some of the more passive, unmechanical activities presently being given the hard sell: Ernest Borgnine, for example, has recently been allowed to assay stamp-collecting on a large scale, and many of the philatelic needs of this country are now in the beefy hands of Mr. Borgnine and others like him. This is why we are treated to such jingoistic commemoratives as "Pond Life—Part of the American Way," and "Prairie Dogs—Rodents of Liberty.")

Never treat a man as if he has chosen a particular hobby *deliberately* in lieu of spending time with *you*. If you really choose to think this, you haven't learned to compromise. Sometimes you can even contrive to spend an entire Saturday with your TOYMAN, if you agree to spend most of the morning kneeling on the living room floor three and three-eighths inches from his right-hand speaker, as he raises and lowers the volume in precise increments, yelling, "*Now* do you hear the hiss I told you about? Wait a minute. . . . *Now* do you hear it?" You don't think he'd choose *anyone* for this role, do you?

Keep this in mind: If a man does not have a noticeable, all-consuming hobby, there is no way of knowing for sure that he is not luring boy scouts into the garage and sharing unwholesome literature with them.

2. The Sports Imperative

Sports, for a man, are rarely a "hobby." They are a way of life.

If, for example, when you first met him, he introduced himself as "a systems analyst, and a left-handed starter with a 10–2 record, nine saves, and eighty-seven career victories," you can probably assume he lives with a high degree of sports awareness.

A man breathes fire when he thinks of sports. He paws the pavement. He feels his oats. He never thinks of his television corner, for example, as a mere cathode-ray tube in a rec room in Cleveland. It is his Dugout. It is his hallowed spot on the Scrimmage Line of life. He dreams of the day a hockey puck will actually sail out of the screen and smash him in the jaw; and when it does, he will wipe the blood off his cheeks and say, "Toots, get me a Miller, okay?"

Just because adherents of the discipline of Sport answer to the names of "Goose," "Skeeter," and "Sparky" does not mean that they are not fine parents and respectable members of the community.

Toleration on your part is called for.

However, man is inherently suspicious of women's participation in the World of Sport. He knows that women have made some modest effort in the area of Team Play for Profit. But he also knows that women have instigated the concept of AEROBIC DANCE as a species of athletic event. He cannot imagine himself, or any other consenting human, in a candy-striped leotard and peach leg warmers, getting Down and Funky with Michael Jackson.

No, a man often feels, rationally or not, that Woman is trying to run blocking strategies between him and his beloved World of Sport, and HE DOES NOT GO FOR THIS. NOT EVEN A LITTLE.

For this reason, never try to threaten a sportsman. His body chemicals are too damn potent. Far too many women have put their little feet down and said, "No more, Dick. It's me or the Celtics." And they find that the next sound they hear is that of their makeup case hitting the front sidewalk. They have made the mistake of forgetting that they can never perform a sexual act in any way comparable to Larry Bird doing a perfect layup under heavy guard, eleven minutes into the fourth quarter, with the score 101–102.

A woman must learn to Go with the Flow (as some non-Sportsman put it once).

Some suggestions:

TURN YOUR HOME INTO A SPORTS HALL OF FAME

Learn to use little pennants as decorating motifs. (If you are in doubt about how to do this, check out Wally Cleaver's bedroom in reruns of the popular "Leave It to Beaver" program.) Offer to have him put you on salary as his PERSONAL SPORTS ARCHIVIST.

TURN YOUR MEALS INTO PLAY-OFFS

This can be lots of fun for both of you.

- Instead of handing him a dinner roll some night, say, "Hey, Steve, heads up. It's first and ten. Drop into the pocket!" And don't give him any butter until he gains some real yardage.
- Draw a festive fifty-yard line down the center of the dining room table. Divide your vegetables into teams: The carrots, for example, can be Ohio State; and the beets can be Northwestern. (Northwestern always loses, even at water polo; and everyone hates beets.)
- Ask your pets if they wouldn't mind doing some blocking or punting.

PLAN YOUR NEXT FIGHT ACCORDING TO NCAA REGULATIONS

Learn how to feint, jab, and hook; how to float like a butterfly and sting like a bee. Buy your loungewear from Everlast; encourage him to Come Out Fighting. Tell him how his Weight Advantage excites you sexually. And it can't hurt to buy a new LOGO BATHROBE that says DR. DESTRUCTO, KILLER BITCH, or MONGO.

These are only suggestions. As the great basketball coach Bobby Knight once said, "LEAD, FOLLOW, OR GET THE HELL OUT OF THE WAY."

This means absolutely nothing. But it does contain profanity, so Sportsmen are fond of repeating it to each other.

3. The Male-Bonding Imperative

As we have seen, a woman cannot expect to fulfill *all* a man's personal needs. A man also needs a sort of "communion," if you will, with members of his own sex.

Male "bonding" is a very beautiful and pure thing. To be able to get together and call each other names like "Moocher" and "Scrotum Head" and "You Old Son of a Bitch" . . . To put out lighted cigarettes on each other's arms . . . To tell jokes about minorities and brag about pulled hamstrings and drunk-driving arrests . . . These special moments are important to a man's sense of self-worth.

The men who made America great were not only great—they were men. They were men who said, "With liberty and justice for all, and hey, Jack, *your money's no good here*, you son of a bitch. *I'm buying*."

Women have never learned to say "I'm buying" with quite the right ring of feigned generosity. "I'm buying" makes men seethe with thrilling hormonal secretions. But when women *should* be saying it, they're saying, "Hey, have you got change for a twenty?" and the moment is gone forever. Or women are saying, "Hey, Betty, did you have the spinach salad or the pita surprise? With tomato that's twenty extra, okay? Not that I'm trying to be cheap."

Women aren't used to carrying rolls of Big Moola around in their pockets. They still pull twenty-dollar bills out of their purses with wonderment, as if Santa had just come to town. If they could *eat* money, they would—not buy rounds of drinks for roomfuls of yahoos who may or may not remember their names the next morning.

It is actually considered *vulgar* for a woman to offer to buy, say, a meal for a whole tableful of men. (It is of course okay for her to offer to *cook* a meal for a whole tableful of men.)

You should never feel jealous or left out if your man wants to spend a lot of time at drinking establishments "powering down brews"; getting tight as an owl; watching wide-screen gridiron events and talking in an extremely loud voice; and getting to know members of his own gender on a more intimate level.

If you *don't* allow him to do these things he will ultimately resent you.

Some men feel they can only express themselves freely in the company of other men: A man needs to feel he has an environment in which he can burp openly and creatively, arm wrestle, risk large sums of money on rigged sporting events, and make jokes about flatulence. (This latter subject causes almost universal revulsion in women and almost universal mirth in men. Television personality ED MCMAHON has been making a living laughing at this type of material for almost a quarter of a century. Clearly, we are talking about an anthropological phenomenon—something to do with Jung's notion of the Collective Unconscious.)

What can women ever expect to know about Male Bonding? *Spit*—that's what. Obviously it's a survival-linked instinct, so messing with it or analyzing it is never wise.

Ignore it, and catch up on your reading.

4. The Trash-Pornography Imperative

The more men are told that they shouldn't enjoy pornography, the more they enjoy it. This is why pornographers can actually sound intelligent when they appear on TV. Anyone who goes up against them sounds like your mother, and the pornographers always win by default.

You may think that pornography is vile, and that any woman named Bambi who likes to spread her legs in public, and says she likes to Do It in an Airplane Restroom With Tall Dark Sagittarians, probably isn't very bright. You may be right, but heaven isn't giving out awards to people like you anymore.

You have to face the fact that most men have some kind of pornography collection—even the ones that say they don't. Even judges. Even FBI agents. Especially FBI agents.

Half the fun in *having* pornography is in hiding it. Even though you always know where he keeps it, it's a bad idea to ruin his fun by letting on that you do.

And there can be pornography right under your very nose that you don't even see. All these things are pornography:

- Anything on cable
- Most of actress CHARLENE TILTON
- Anything by a writer named Dirck
- Anything your man keeps in a sock drawer that isn't a sock
- The annual *Sports Illustrated* bathing-suit issue

Modern pornography, as we know it, was invented in sixteenth-century Delft, the Netherlands, by enterprising coffee merchants, who saw a great need for visual stimulation among the dockworkers of the Low Countries. They paid local maidens and fishwives twelve guilders an hour to lower their bodices and say "Boopty-Boopty" in a provocative sort of way. In the years since, men of varying nationalities and professions have fallen into the tight, swollen grip of pornography, and become stuck, there for better or for worse. Some men like their pornography light and sparkling; but the vast majority cast their vote for "noisome, retch-inducing trash," and plenty of it. (Pornography intended for women has always been bewildering—except, perhaps, to its creators. Pages and pages of hirsute gentlemen waving their gonads in the breeze while 1) speedboating in the Everglades, 2) lubing their MGBs, 3) shot-putting, 4) ordering milkshakes—in other words, nudity just as you encounter it in your day-to-day life. But then, pornography for women is produced on the West Coast, where even No Parking zones are considered erogenous.)

"Why do men *enjoy* pornography?" many have asked. At least *real* women are 3-D—at least they *breathe* in the right places during sex—at least real women seem to enhance the vast number of sexual experiences that men can have.

But when a man sees a woman in a magazine impaling herself on a peeled cucumber, he knows he will not have to say things to her like, "Do you work around here?" He can have a relationship with her without having to have his blazer pressed.

A man's relationship with his pornography collection is highly personal. A lot of thoughtful man-hours have gone into its selection and perusal. Like as not, he's kept it lovingly preserved (much like his frag mug and his catcher's mitt from high school).

If your mind is full of nagging questions about the moral justification of pornography, don't ask them. He can't give you an intellectual answer. We are talking about the preservation of his most secret soul here. You have to be named "Tiffany" or "Suzette" to understand the intricacies involved.

2

Man
in the Home

NEATSTYLES

NOWADAYS, we have more than just *life styles*. We have *NeatStyles*. Meaning that all couples are Odd Couples deep down. No two people ever have the same ideas about how often to take out the trash, how often to dry-clean the slip-covers, how many fingerprints on a windowpane definitively constitute "filth."

You are either a Felix or an Oscar in this life, and one can never understand the other, despite love, friendship, therapy, and lecturing. If you are considering settling in with an Extreme Case, however, you may need special counsel.

The Extremely Sloppy Man

The first thing we need to ask is, "Can the human trash heap be retrained, or is it congenital?"

There is evidence that sloppiness is controlled by the left side of the brain, and that there are certain behavior patterns that accompany the trait: A sloppy man will never leave a half-filled juice glass by the bed, if he can also put out a cigarette in it and leave *that* in the glass. For at least a week. Sometimes a dead fly will fall in the glass to keep the cigarette company. Sloppy men like this sort of thing: They tend to be very sociable people.

There are also a number of theories stating that sloppiness in a man is environmentally engendered. The most popular theory revolves around the years he spent watching

Saturday morning cartoons while his mother vacuumed around his feet, saying, "Don't move. Is the noise disturbing you, Baby?"

Growing up, most men did not suffer adverse peer pressure about being sloppy. They would invite their friends over to watch the tube on top of a stack of fermenting athletic supporters, and they would use their wall-light fixtures as combination coat-and-towel racks, and they would watch bizarre mold cultures literally *consume* their bedroom rug at the alarming rate (someone once clocked this) of three centimeters a day. They did not apologize for this. This was cool.

But let's pay a visit to the full-grown sloppy man at the moment in history when you are actually deciding whether you should live with him, and let's see what makes him run:

- A very sloppy man *has* furniture, but it's been so long since he's seen it, he couldn't necessarily identify it in a police lineup. (*"That's my couch.* No, wait a minute— maybe it was beige.")

- Sloppy men do not *worry* about things. That's why they drive you crazy. They write themselves notes on the back of takeout Chinese menus. If they can read these notes a week later through the duck sauce, fine. If not, what's to get excited about?

- Sloppy men are popular with their peers, since they never make their peers look bad. They're very good-natured and always look a little gassed-up. It is possible that they've left the stove on, or that they've just smelled their towels.

- Before he met you, the sloppy man very likely had a "girl" who came in with reinforcements of Bab-O and so on, to try to clear a space for him in the detritus of his life. Take this woman for a drink. She knows more about him than most of his old girlfriends do.

- A very sloppy man does not so much have "rooms" as "habitation quadrants." As long as he can find his television, he has a place in the universe. The television provides order. It has commercials at regular intervals. It has people in neat clothes who express their continued desire for the whitener in Final Touch. Even the test pattern consists of straight lines. They soothe him. They tell him *someone* is out there neatening things up. Just so it doesn't have to be he.

You will understandably be concerned about whether there can be a place for you in one of the sloppy man's habitation quadrants, or whether you'll just have to take a number and wait around for all eternity, or at least until he can *find* you.

It's not as bad as all that. You *can* learn a sloppy man's filing system without a great deal of trouble. He has an "A" pile (his shirts, business letters, Arbyburger wrappers, fish food); a "B" pile (foreign newspapers, athletic shorts, Kleenexes he's saving for recycling); and an "organic pile" (loosely classified as "waste" or even "garbage," except that he liberally spreads it throughout his dwelling, figuring it'll get lonely in the corner all by itself).

A sloppy man also has closets but not in the sense that most ordinary humans think of "closets." This man heard, in the late sixties, about the concept of "time capsules"—in which copies of *The New York Times* and Chuck Berry records were sent into outer space for the reading and dancing pleasure of aliens throughout the cosmos. And so he too is accumulating, *in his closet,* a unique record of his terrestrial existence. He doesn't have to put a sign on his closet saying "Do Not Open Until 1991." You should simply *know* better.

"How can I occupy the same space, comfortably, with my man?" many have asked. "Space" is indeed the key word. If the two of you lived in a forty-three-room apartment, he could be messy in his space and you could be neat in your space, and you would only have to get together, for sex and brunches, on weekends.

But space, like matter, is disappearing from the universe at an appreciable rate. *Better Homes and Gardens* will someday be *Better Closets and Windowboxes.* Perhaps someday a device will be invented that will facilitate *molecular transfer,* so that two masses will be able to occupy the same space at the same time. You'll be able to sit on the same couch, take the same shower, groom at the same mirror, and *you* will not even be able to see the fossilized hero sandwich he has for some reason left sitting on the dining room table for the last three weeks.

Until that day, though, you can take only small, *practical* steps toward coexisting with your human slimeball. Foremost, you should bear in mind that there are many worse things in this world than living with a high-maintenance man. Seriously, much, much worse. You *could* end up living with

The Terminally Tidy Man.

Very sloppy men aren't at all secretive about their habits. But very neat men are sort of like pederasts or Mafiosi or ax murderers—the neighbors almost invariably *think* they're normal. And this fate could befall you, too.

You may someday meet a man with agreeably razor-creased trousers and an aura of crisp, minty-fresh orderliness about him; a man spotless in both reputation and bathroom Formica. And you may want this man. You cannot be faulted for this.

Like many, you may feel that a Very Neat Man is a kindred spirit to a Very Neat Woman. But a Very Neat Woman is just an ordinary, well-meaning anal-compulsive sap who's been taught to shake the crumbs out of the bed linen because, good gosh, who else is going to do it?

A Very Neat Man is from Mars.

And you'll know from the moment you visit his home whether he's One of Them:

- There will be labels on all his kitchen cabinets. Typed.
- There will be Airwick refills in the spot where most normal men keep their pornography.
- There will be no fingerprints anywhere in the house, because he *has* no fingerprints.

The Very Neat Man will view you with suspicion, almost from the very beginning. He doesn't really care what you do on *your* time in your *own* apartment, but when you come to visit him, he will frisk you at the door for concealed lint. His eyes will mercilessly follow you around the room, making sure you do not leave unsightly heel marks on his parquet floors, enjoy a light snack without benefit of napkins and coasters, breathe heavily on his stereo turntable, or peruse one of his magazines without putting it back at a ninety-degree angle to the edge of the coffee table.

How do Neat Men get so neat? Can they be trained to be useful members of society before society flees from them with high-pitched squeals and great gnashing of teeth? Can they be persuaded not to vacuum in front of guests, not to wash dishes *during* meals, not to Windex the TV screen after each day's viewing, not to develop allergies to dust, imagined dust, and even theoretical dust?

They will not (research has found) and *cannot* ever change completely. The Very Neat Fellow, when he was a tyke, wanted to grow up to be the Ty-D-bol man and speedboat around in a little toilet dispensing therapeutic chemicals while wearing an admiral's hat and white duck trousers. When he grew a little older, he discovered women, and he marveled to think that there could be activities in life he'd enjoy more than staying home ironing his underwear and flossing between his molars. Some psychologists will tell you that this man became Neat in the first place because of sexual guilt. He may have come to view women's bodies as unclean (and first thing in the morning, very badly pressed).

The Neat Man sleeps terribly and has terrifying dreams about accidentally laundering colors with whites and allowing his phonograph records to be placed back in the rack out of alphabetical order. He may awaken in the middle of the night and rerinse the supper dishes. He may awaken you and ask you if you washed out the bathroom basin after you used it. If you say yes, he will ask you if you dried it.

If you really want to get through to a Very Neat Man, you have to make your point in some often-brutal ways—deliberately kicking a corner of a throw rug out of alignment to see how long he can carry on a conversation without leaping up and righting it again. Or impregnating all his woolens with nasty Static Cling.

There is nothing you can do, you know, to change an anal-compulsive man, since *you,* according to him, are the one with the "Problem." Learn to live with him. And you can: A Very Neat Man has a lot of things going for him, if you can get past the more obvious trials. You will never have to do housework again, because he will not *allow* you to, even if you beg.

And he will never, never mess around with other women. It's too messy.

BATHROOMS

PEOPLE carry a lot of Bathroom Myths around with them from childhood. Stories, for example, that many of the following can be transmitted on bathroom towels: plantar's warts, piles, shingles, viral pneumonia, Down's syndrome, Burkitt's lymphoma, common colds, unusual colds, really strange colds, and Huntington's chorea.

These stories are of course ridiculous. You cannot get shingles from bathroom towels.

It is a good idea, when you and your man are first living together, to actually *write down* a bathroom schedule, stating
• realistic bathroom needs
• realistic time limits
• responsibility for periodic cleaning, maintenance, etc.

This list will give you something to laugh at in the years to come.

Here are the important components of a well-run bathroom and some suggestions as to their use.

The Medicine Cabinet

The Berlin Wall was but a mad whim compared with most medicine cabinet demarcations. People get territorial about their toilet items. And there is some logic at work here: It is true that if you touch a razor blade not belonging to you, you will contract a deadly rash and die within forty-eight hours.

At least you, as a *woman*, understand what a man does with most of his personal hygiene products. He kills bacteria, removes extremely basic hair growths, and lathers whatever is momentarily unclean. That's it.

But there are things about your self-care regimen that scare men to death. Your body is like Nepal to him—on a higher plane, mystical, locus of secret ceremonies going back before the dawn of his existence. You have rubber items that may be inserted into the body, or one which may be flange fittings for a Toyota. He can never really be sure.

Why, a man wonders, do women's toilet products always have a cylindrical shape with a rounded tip, and squirt out some kind of viscous, pearly liquid? A man feels like an interloper in the presence of these items.

And he has other questions, too: Why are women's toiletries always named in such a way that you can never figure out what they *do*? Is Lancome's Nourishing Hydrating Emulsion something you rub on, something you bathe in, or something you drink? What is it that is done by Chanel's *Crème Extrême Protection* and Evian's *Brumisateur Hydration* that cannot adequately be explained in English? If you are using Clinique's 7th-Day Scrub Cream, WHAT ARE YOU DOING ON THE OTHER SIX DAYS THAT HE DOESN'T KNOW ABOUT?

This is why it's important to take him by the hand occasionally and explain to him that you need certain chemical preparations to retain your youthful, vibrant glow; and that through the years, you are going to (1) take him by the hand more often, (2) age, and accordingly (3) demand more shelf space.

Shower/Bathtub

If the medicine cabinet is the woman's bailiwick, the shower stall is the man's. If you are living with a sportsman, he takes lots and lots of showers. At least three times a day. Since his body is his temple, he frequently has religious visions in the shower.

Men who sing in the shower are like men who snore—if that's the worst thing you can say about them, then you oughtn't to be grousing.

Dancing in the shower is a bit more serious, but as long as he doesn't wear taps, you do not have any major cause for complaint.

Since ancient times, it has traditionally been the lot of women to remove grime and sediment from bathtub surfaces. Women do not seem to be more biologically equipped to clean bathtubs (unless it's that they have a lower center of gravity), but they have consistently drawn the short straw when it comes to the Bathtub Sweepstakes, and things seem unlikely to change.

Cleaning a bathtub is not an act you can enter into casually, with a soft drink in your hand or while standing up. Rather, you must gird yourself with kneepads and various weapons of assault, like a goalie for the Maple Leafs. (You might even try this interesting SPORTS METAPHOR on your man. It ought to elicit a chuckle out of him. You'll still end up cleaning the bathtub, but at least you'll have elicited a chuckle.)

Sink

Possibly you remember that in *Last Tango in Paris,* Marlon Brando said that sharing a sink was what kept a lot of marriages together in the days of yore. And you note, with some vexation, that the practice seems to be having the opposite effect in your relationship.

You must bear in mind that Marlon Brando said a lot of things in *Last Tango in Paris.* He also did a lot of things in *Last Tango in Paris;* possibly you remember what they were. There are role models in this life, after all, and there are *role models.*

A clean, sparkling bathroom basin has been the ideal of the American woman since the dawn of the industrialized society. But lately that dream has been in no small jeopardy.

Shaving creams have undergone a revolution. When the new GREEN GELS harden, they cannot be removed from sink enamel except with a blowtorch or small laser gun. (Future civilizations will be able to study your joint history in great detail by excavating layers of shaving gel from your sink.) You must be vigilant, but you must not set unduly high standards of bathroom basin maintenance. If you ever see anything green growing on the north side of your sink, and you're not sure whether it's shaving gel deposits or reindeer moss, *then* you have something to worry about.

Toilets

First of all, if you have been living with a man for more than a year and you still fall into the toilet in the middle of the night because he's left the seat up, then you need this book more than you thought you did, and you'll probably need to read the sequel, too.

A man and his toilet are companions through life's thicks and thins, enjoying a bond that you will never truly understand. He puts a lot of time, effort, and imagination into his man/toilet relationship, and you should respect him for this. Have you been yelling and nitpicking at him through the bathroom door? Have you been advising him to read *shorter* works of literature while in the bathroom, in order to avoid hemorrhoids, muscle atrophy, and worse? Have you been trying to woo him out with reason, physiological truths, idle threats, and niggling, inflammatory questions?

Leave the guy be. Give him his space. If you ever see him taking Tolkien into the bathroom to read, he's not going to settle for less than the entire "Rings" trilogy, so you'll have to cancel all his appointments until Washington's Birthday. But that's a small price to pay for his inner peace.

KITCHEN DETAILS

ALL the great chefs in the world are men. And yet most of the humans laboring at this instant in the kitchens of the world are women.

Maybe you've tried to rectify this statistic and lure him in a kitchenward direction. And maybe his disasters have been costly: He incinerated thirty dollars worth of enoki mushrooms, or all of the Tupperware.

There's a reason for this: MEN DON'T USE COOKBOOKS.

They have no objection to the idea of learning to cook, as long as they don't have to start at the beginning. That means looking at a cookbook. And, COOKBOOKS ARE FOR SISSIES.

Did you ever look at the way a cookbook is written?

It is always *barking* something at you. "*Purée* this," it says. "*Sauté* this." "*Preheat* that."

The average man looks at this sort of thing and says, "Oh, yeah? Who's going to make me?"

Women are used to being ordered around by inanimate things like books. But what a man needs is a cookbook that speaks his language. Something that meets him halfway. Something that doesn't make him feel like a trapped animal.

If you've *both* had a hard day at the office, and you'd like *him* to make the dinner, you could try leaving out some of your favorite recipes in the following BIG-BUSINESS manner:

- "Our cooking success could be firmed up by the inclusion of a half cup of heavy cream."
- "There is strong endorsement for the utilization of swivel-bladed vegetable scrapers, vis-à-vis various eggplants, new potatoes, endives, and Chinese turnips."
- "Market research has indicated that there is strong public identification with ½ clove garlic, salt and pepper to taste, and 4 cups fresh or canned beef broth."

This is a clear, concise *man-talk* kind of recipe style, and should have him overworking himself in the kitchen in no time.

But cookbooks only tell half the story. Men do like preparing certain *nonrecipe* foods, although they can be easily intimidated by snafus in the preparation procedure. Take hard-boiling an egg:

A man who's never boiled an egg before admires the integrity of an egg. It's white and smooth and doesn't bother anybody. . . . And then, lo and behold, it *cracks* on him.

The first time this happens, he will call to you in the other room. "Oh my God, it's *breaking*," he will say. "What shall I do?"

Now, there's a question. What shall he do? Here he is looking at a half ounce of white, semiliquid protein that all the laws of physics can't put back together again, and you'd darn well better believe that he sees it as a reflection on his masculinity.

When a woman boils an egg and it breaks, she believes it's her fault. She picked the *defective model*, out of a possible roster of twelve. When a man looks at a broken egg, he feels he should be able to put it back together again.

This is when you need to pull *him* together; to tell him them's the breaks, so to speak. Tell him that eggs have been breaking on women for centuries, but women, being genetically related to eggs, can understand this. (Men think women are more spiritual than they are, anyway. They're secretly jealous of this quality. You should use it more often.)

Men seem to like preparing breakfast on a weekend, and they can make a big production out of it, making little origami pickup trucks out of the napkins, incorporating birthday candles into the bacon omelette, creating a *theme table* with coordinated paper plates and coffee mugs. They look very shy while in the midst of these proceedings—the heat of the stove makes their eyelashes curl, and they perspire ever so slightly (not like in sports but just in a very adorable, barely moist way).

They like salads, too. No one can tell them they're doing a salad *wrong*. It can't burn or run or fall or curdle or whistle at them.

Most of all, though, men like cooking anything that bleeds. It's very manly.

This is why men have always been avid barbecuers. Barbecuing is taming another formerly *living* thing into submission—or at least into juicy, toothsome pinkness, a little seared on the outside. A barbecuing man is a 3-D, *performing* man. An action guy. He lights potent fires, orders people around, pokes his cow flesh with a long-handled fork, and wears a manly-looking full-length apron that tells everyone in six-inch letters exactly how terrific he is. And if they're in doubt about this latter truth, he tells them: "All *right*—who's ready for some *monster* steaks here? Who's ready for some *monster* enjoyment? Who's ready to die and go to heaven?" (A man tends to use violent metaphors to connote enjoyment. It's nothing for you to worry about as long as he's in a BARBECUE MODE.)

You had better believe, too, that barbecuing is a PSYCHO-SEXUAL RITUAL. His public performance at the grill is a public reflection on him and on you. Do you want it known (he feels) that you live and eat and bed with a man whose BRIQUETTES repeatedly WON'T LIGHT?

It is debatable whether there will ever really be room in the kitchen for both of you.

What is "cooking" after all?

When it comes right down to it, it was probably a woman who thought up the nicety of buying a meat or vegetable, cooking it up on a stove, serving it on a plate at an appointed hour, and having a nice conversation while consuming it.

Men are all enthused about the *idea* of the above, but left to their own devices, they frequently revert to allowing a bowl of fudge ripple ice cream to serve as an entire meal—allowing the bowl to sit at room temperature, then mushing the ice cream around until it turns medium beige, then letting it dribble off the spoon.

"Eccch," you say to him. "Is that the kind of thing you'd do at *home*?" And then you realize he *is* home.

Think about this. It's very profound.

THE VERMIN ISSUE

THINGS frequently crawl into people's homes, and someone has to do something about them. And most women do just about everything in their power to make sure it isn't *them*.

Some see this as a sexist issue. After all, man does not have to fell all the timber anymore, and woman does not *have* to churn the cheese. But women seem not to have changed a whit in the area of Extremely Gross Insect disposal.

"OH MY GOD! COME HERE QUICK! IT'S GOT FOUR HUNDRED LEGS AND IT'S THE SIZE OF TORONTO!"

We expect men to hear these words and come running with swords drawn, a look of divine vengeance transforming their otherwise wholesome features.

Why do we think men enjoy this?

Inwardly, they are Jell-o at these times. Many urgent and troublesome questions pass through their brains.

- "What if it secretes poison gasses?"
- "Will a back issue of *Natural History* kill it, and what if I want to read it afterward?"

And most importantly,

- "How do I know if it's dead? What if it's Just Kidding?"

Even after nuclear war, when people will become just as dead as it is humanly possible to be, many species of bugs will be Just Kidding.

They will wipe themselves off, tip their little hats to each other, and erect little tent cities in the remains of your bathroom.

Due to the miracle of genetic engineering, Extremely Gross Insects have a generational turnover rate of once every six hours. Certain larvae can become grandparents by the time you've had your 3 P.M. coffee break.

For this reason, we need men more than ever.

We need men to flush the Bugparts down the toilet. (And, as they enter the sewer system, each Bugpart spontaneously reproduces, and then all the Parts come back and Find You, because your plumbing is all clearly labeled in Bug Language. And at a prearranged time, all the Bugparts crawl out of the drain and say, "Boo! Remember me?" And who's going to put *you* back together, if not a man?)

THE PLACE OF WIT IN THE AMERICAN HOME

IF you ever read the Bachelor-of-the-Month column in *Cosmopolitan,* you know what luscious hunks like BURT REYNOLDS, JAMES CAAN, and JOE NAMATH appreciate most in a woman: a sense of humor.

They always say this. And not just because it's crude to say, "I go for giganto tits" in a national publication. Men really do respect and appreciate a sense of humor in a woman.

So it's important for you to cultivate one. But (and this is an important "but") make sure it's the right *kind:*

A woman with a good sense of humor is not a woman who makes jokes.

A woman with a good sense of humor is a woman who *laughs* at jokes.

It doesn't matter if you have the soul of Voltaire, S. J. Perelman, and Jan Murray all rolled into one: MAKING JOKES AROUND THE HOUSE WILL GET YOU IN TROUBLE. IT WILL NOT MAKE YOU POPULAR.

Don't you remember how your mother used to say to you, "Don't get *funny* with me, young lady." She was trying to prepare you for your life with a man.

If you're a jokey sort of person, trust me on this one: Next time you feel the urge to get funny—especially funnier than *he* is, BAG IT. Go into the bathroom, lock the door, and practice saying "These two flamingos walked into a bar" in the mirror until you get it out of your system.

Women who get funny during fights are in especially big trouble. You may *think,* for example, that you've just whipped off the best one-liner ever heard in the continental U.S. since Jack Benny's old radio show. A man—any man —will always have the same thing to say in reply.

"I see. So now we're getting sarcastic."

You may see Joan Rivers being sarcastic on television, but she has better clothes than you do.

Dorothy Parker was very sarcastic, but it made her an alcoholic. Or maybe it was the other way around. Anyway, she's dead.

Jane Austen was sarcastic, but she was a man.

Occasionally you can get away with saying something very witty around the house, if you can make him think (even temporarily) that someone *else* said it first.

He will stop in his tracks with a gleam of guarded amusement in his eye. "Hm-m," he will muse. "That sounds familiar. Did Somebody say that once?"

"Yes," you confess. "*I* just said it. Just now. That was *me* talking."

Of course, it'll all be over at this point—he'll mutter something like, "*Bartlett's Quotations* ought to include a footnote about 'Famous Suburban Household Wits,'" and that will be the end of your place in the Comedy Sun.

It almost sounds as if funniness is all tied up with masculinity here. Well, it *is*. A man KNOWS "funny." A man "knows" for example that BOB HOPE is funny. (Bob Hope hasn't actually *been* funny since the Allies liberated Guadalcanal; nor was he *particularly* funny even then, but people were all caught up in patriotic hysteria.) A number of men —especially Frenchmen—feel that JERRY LEWIS is funny. (And yet you know that ten million Frenchmen can't be intelligent.)

A Funny Guy is definitely popular among other guys:
• Funny Guys never have to buy their own Molsons.
• Funny Guys get invited to bachelor parties and poker nights and hunting lodges.
• Whenever guys go out to do Guy Things, they bring Funny Guys with them.

A Funny Guy *is* Guy-dom. He is the seven-hundred-pound stag on the deer rack of life.

And you cannot hope to be a part of this. Imagine yourself walking into the middle of a poker night saying, "Excuse me, guys—anyone like some more Cheetos? And by the way, *these two midgets were walking down the street. . . .*"

BAG IT.

I'm telling you.

SLEEPING TOGETHER

ONCE you are officially living with a man, "sleeping together" may or may not have something to do with sex.

More often, it has something to do with issues like territoriality, internal clocks, REM cycles, somnambulism, and body heat diffusion. It is only in commercials for Paco Rabanne cologne that couples argue adorably about snoring and who stole the covers. In real life, these can be ugly, vitriol-stained issues.

Sleep Needs

Sleep needs are different for men and women. Men need more sleep than women; they are more athletic sleepers, they can perform more feats of strength, breathe more deeply, and jump higher during sleep than women can. Men need more sleep immediately after sex, and occasionally during sex, than women do.

The most striking sex differences are in the area of dreams. Women dream in more vivid colors than men do, but men have more of a capacity to dream, and conceptualize, in 3-D. (So that when they go to the movies, they don't *really* have to wear those fruity cardboard glasses.)

Women tend to dream more about family life, gardening, knitting, cooking, driving around in circles, begging their way out of traffic tickets, and menstruating.

Men tend to dream about bullfighting, cockfighting, harpooning whales, stock car racing, having sex with prostitutes, and driving through tunnels.

Men achieve erections while they are dreaming, known to clinicians as "waking up in a tent." Men, like hamsters, if awakened during a dream, will attempt to have intercourse with the nearest member of the same species, unless they are doused with water, or shown photographs of aggressive or undesirable-looking hamsters, or hamsters with large hindsections.

Men who cannot sleep never fail to remind you of the household tasks they performed the night before. They bathed the dog, changed fuses, performed carpentry jobs, counted ceiling tiles, counted grooves on automobile tires, built sets of dining room furniture, counted to three hundred in sevens, and cleaned out the refrigerator (not the dirt—just the food).

Snoring

Snoring was invented by God for a reason. Learning to love a man's deviated septum is an exercise in Christian charity.

Most men only snore in a particular position. Whatever that position is, it is the only one you will be physically unable to move him out of.

Men snore in cycles. They usually begin with a noise like a load of coal tumbling down a chute, then switch to an interesting chainsaw effect, then move up to something not unlike a Pittsburgh steel mill just before quitting time. Then they wake themselves up and start the cycle anew.

If you read the popular ANN LANDERS column, you know what your reaction to this syndrome should be: "Well, things could be worse. At least I know he hasn't *died* in the middle of the night." (The popular ANN LANDERS often uses guilt to make her points.)

Over the years, humanity has tried to come up with cures for snoring. Surgery, Hypnosis. Hanging amulets from the bedpost. Buddhist chanting. Painting the bedroom therapeutic colors. Shouting and screaming. Sticking needles under his fingernails. Things of this nature. But a *cure*, per se, has never been found.

Do men know they're snoring while they're snoring? On some level, they must. And on some level they are saying to themselves, "Well, things could be worse. At least I know I haven't *died* in the middle of the night." (Men also read the popular ANN LANDERS column.)

Old men are not the only ones who snore. Dishy men snore, too. (They snore dishily, but they snore.) And it is only a myth that men of the Hebraic and Italianate cultures snore because of relative nose size. Italianate men snore as a sign of fertility. Hebraic men snore as a way of saying, "Things could be worse. I *could* have . . ."

You get the idea.

Somehow *related* to snoring (though scientists don't know how) is the habit men have of rolling over on you like a beached whale and sweating on you in the middle of the night. This is known as "unconditional love." You shouldn't be complaining about it.

There are some issues you will *never* be able to hammer out a solution to, as a couple, because you are two different people; and everyone thinks he sleeps, if not *better,* then at least *smarter* than the next person.

- ARGUING ABOUT WHO STOLE THE COVERS is common among people who are very territorial in bed. You might consider hiring an impartial observer to spend the night in your room and determine who in fact *did* steal the covers, how many times it happened, whether it was motivated by greed or hypothermia, and whether action should be brought against the offender. This is pretty picayune stuff, but even famous movie stars probably argue about it, although they get to do it with a wider selection of people.

- ARGUING ABOUT KEEPING THE WINDOW OPEN is a close second in popularity. Some people (usually men) like to have that sash open a crack to create the impression of an exhilarating, windswept night camping in the Rockies. In fact, burglars apprehended after breaking into such homes have often stated that they were seeking "the impression of an exhilarating, windswept night camping in the Rockies." Women who are always cold and like to keep the windows shut have prevented innumerable crimes in our society.

- WAKING TIME: Some men like to get up early, while the birdies are still cheeping and dawn is stealing wraithlike across the lawn and you're still dreaming about accidentally finding Harrison Ford's wallet and having to deliver it to him in person in a steambath. These men tend to be quite productive, running seventy or so miles before breakfast, playing twelve or thirteen games of Missile Command on their Ataris, reading and proofreading the local newspapers, and downing a gallon or so of coffee.

A great many men, though, enjoy languishing in dreamland *(where you can't get at them)* as long as humanly possible.

Many women do not realize that SLEEPING MEN ARE A GREAT NATURAL RESOURCE, and right under our collective noses, too.

You can get a man to do almost anything by talking to him while he is asleep. Most women who have lived with men a long time realize that not talking to men while they are sleeping is a waste of valuable time. So what if they can't hear you? When men are asleep

- They don't interrupt.
- They don't say, "Whose moronic idea was that? Your mother's?"
- They can't walk out of the room.
- They can't accuse you of never discussing it with them first.
- They can't roll their eyes in disgust (not even during REM cycles).

Your mother has been talking to your father in his sleep for years, but it never occurred to her to pass on this trick to you because, like her recipe for deviled tuna-in-a-doughhole, she always just took it for granted.

Here are some things that have been successfully said to sleeping men in the past:

- "I'm taking eighty-five dollars out of your wallet now, okay?"
- "I'm throwing away all your letters from that dyed-blond bitch Sheila now, okay?"
- "I think we should start a family soon. Like in about five minutes now. Okay?"

Most men, when they've awakened, will not remember your conversation. They may have had vague dreams about having been assaulted by woodpeckers, but the gist of the conversation is embedded safely in their subconscious. You feel satisfied.

THE SLEEPING-WITH-A-MAN FILM FESTIVAL

ONE of the fun by-products of sleeping together is staying up late and watching TV in bed. Midnight news wrap-ups, for example, have become popular of late: Some women cannot slumber without bearing witness, yet again, to the winsome crinkles that form around Ted Koppel's eyes when union spokesmen are lying to him. This sort of thing wears thin with men pretty quickly.

Classic Old Movies are usually highly acceptable to both men and women, but who makes the selection is a perennial problem.

If you're smart, you'll let him choose most of the time. He'll just fall asleep during your ("too sentimental") selections anyway, and the next morning say something like, "If Bette Davis really had that brian tumor, how did she light all those cigarettes without setting her face on fire?"

There are certain movies that men never want to miss, no matter how many times they've seen them. Your man will feel very "close" to you if you share them with him, and also keep your mouth shut at the right times. Any Charles Bronson movie falls into the "must-see" category. Only a guy like Bronson could have carried off something like the famous "Family Jewels" scene in *The Valachi Papers*. (Where Bronson mercifully kills his best friend, who's just been castrated by the Mafia. Compared with castration, most men feel that death is merely Highly Unpleasant.)

Here is a sampling of men's favorite movies.

Forbidden Planet

One of the greatest science-fiction movies ever made, it has at least four major virtues: (1) electronic music (in *1956*),

(2) a really splendid robot, and (3) and (4) the breasts of Anne Francis. (The last two will grow progressively more interesting as he grows older.)

In this film, a bunch of astronauts lands on a planet ruled by Walter Pidgeon (in a very expensive black bathrobe), and this "Dr. Morbeus" behaves very oddly and coldly (hence the MOVIE'S TITLE) because he knows something the astronauts don't: There are MONSTERS loose on the planet, but they're not dumb, fake-looking 1956 movie monsters. They're MONSTERS FROM THE ID. (That's right, as in "The Ego and————.") And there follows a well-paced war of wills (yes, and ray guns too), and I won't tell you what happens, but Anne Francis's costume really gets a workout, and so will your man.

The Adventures of Robin Hood

Some men literally fall in love with Errol Flynn in this movie, and not just because he's wearing tights.

Men love the idea of a bunch of guys living in the forest, outside the law, eating mutton haunches, and throwing the bones on the ground. (Belching was not allowed in the movies under the Hayes Act, or men would have enjoyed seeing that, too.)

There is a classic swordfight at the climax of this movie between Basil Rathbone and Errol Flynn, where Flynn slices the tops off candles with his sword and leaves them still burning.

At the end of this movie, Robin Hood gets the King of England's express permission to go off in a turret somewhere and Seriously Mess Around with Olivia de Havilland, who was the most notoriously insipid movie virgin of the thirties. This was probably some kind of movie first, although Mr. Flynn's lower costume never betrays any particular enthusiasm.

Angels with Dirty Faces

The whole point of this film is the scene where Cagney goes to the chair. *Never talk during this part of the movie.* Too many women have been thrown out of households on their ear for talking or asking point-of-reference questions during the scene where Cagney goes to the chair. Too many of them say, "So what? I'd get hysterical too if I was gonna *fry*."

In point of fact, women who overanalyze Cagney films deserve a grapefruit in the face.

The Magnificent Seven

This movie has everything: seven of the greatest tough-guy actors ever assembled in one Western, most particularly Steve ("We deal in lead, friend") McQueen.

This movie has a heart: Noble Gunmen out to protect impoverished village from Evil Bandits who wear suspiciously large souvenir sombreros.

It has James Coburn picking off an enemy rider from three hundred yards away, and saying, "Shoot. I was aiming for the *horse*."

It has Elmer Bernstein's exciting theme music, which was later used to sell billions of Marlboro cigarettes.

It's a movie where a lot of crusty, trail-hardened guys discover the meaning of honor by blowing away Eli Wallach for talking with such a terrible Mexican accent.

It had at least forty-three sequels. Shoot, it deserved them.

Any Unusually Gross Horror Movie

Men have always liked horror movies better than women. And male horror fans can become rather irritating when they try to "convert" you and you don't want to be converted. Not even *ever*. When you're in the kitchen quietly puking your guts out over something you've just seen on the TV screen, he's calling you from the other room: "Come here, honey! You're missing the tractor-trailer running over the festering body parts!"

Some have said that horror movies are CATHARTIC. Better to be afraid of 173 pounds of synthetic slime on a movie screen than to have it visit *your* neighborhood. But this theory has never been clinically proven, and thus gross horror films are the one part of the Sleeping-with-a-Man Film Festival from which you may legitimately be excused.

Some people, it seems, *like* to be scared. (Some people like to be buried alive in pickle relish and stomped on by dwarfs. There's no accounting for taste.)

Any Badly Dubbed Martial Arts Film from Hong Kong or Taiwan

Most martial-arts extravaganzas are filmed in the Orient, because the scenery is beautiful, extras are cheap, life is cheap, and everyone already wears one-size-fits-all white kung fu pajamas.

Fights to the death often break out inexplicably during meals in martial arts films, and everyone throws a lot of dishes (often with food still in them, which can be very upsetting for women to watch).

The plots of these films usually revolve around gangs of thugs who go around leveling their daunting Fists of Terror against innocent citizenry (usually in restaurants, so there will be enough dishes to throw). You can distinguish the thugs from the heroes because the thugs have latex scars, grunt when they eat, and are Impolite to Maidens.

Martial arts antagonists numb their opponents most usually by leaping through the air feet first, smashing masonry, and screaming terrifyingly—no body contact actually occurs, but many people die from the *psychological effects* of all the leaping and screaming; many citizens end up splayed on the ground with large ketchup stains on their pajamas. Most characters in martial arts films get killed and maimed several times, but virtue always triumphs in the end.

No one knows who replaces the dishes, or why people in violence-ridden areas of the Orient don't have the sense to use paper plates.

PETS

THERE is no doubt that a jolly little PET can add dimension to your life together. Even if it's very small, any four-legged domestic mammal skittering around your house is bound to affect your relationship in *some* way.

But it could be adversely. The same man who would never admit to hating a child, or even a wallpaper pattern, feels no compunctions whatever about energetically loathing the cherished pet you've brought into your common home. Conversely, he can fall madly in love with some wretched, dippy mutt who regularly gets Irritable Bowel Syndrome in your shoe closet—no explanations, no apologies.

A Pet is like a Rorschach test—the way a person reacts to a certain kind of pet says a lot about his or her character. It is important, therefore, to know *why* your man has certain Pet Preferences.

Fish

I thought about including fish in the Toys section of this book.

No man really *likes* fish. Not personally, anyway.

A man likes fish *equipment.* He likes the tank, and the tank aerator, and the automatic tank sterilizer, and most of all he likes the little plastic deep-sea diver that stands on the bottom of the tank. (See, he feels he *is* this guy, sort of looking out at himself through the glass. Pretty strange, *non?*)

Canines

Dogs exert an irresistible, and not entirely healthy, pull on men. Certain qualities in dog-dom induce men to become sentimental sops, often much to your amazement: The same man who can sit through BARBARA STANWYCK'S greatest cinematic efforts without any adverse effect whatever on the tear ducts will become a pile of mush over some old episode of *Lassie*. (The blue mange attacks Lassie's hometown, and she has to stay overnight in a kennel with sadistic Labradors —that sort of thing.)

A man and his dog can gang up on you.

There are many reasons for this:

• A man's dog has never bugged him about putting his shoes on the bed.

• A man's dog has never made unfavorable comparisons between his mother and various Libyan politicians.

• A man's dog has never stopped him as he was leaving the house, saying, "Listen, I think we'd better talk about something *now*."

A dog is everything you are not. He enjoys taking orders from male humans. (In fact the only male human who has been known to enjoy taking orders from a dog was noted Son of Sam killer DAVID BERKOWITZ. But they've got *him* stashed away somewhere safe. I think.)

A dog gratefully accepts everything that is given to him. He does not examine a gift of, say, a Milk-Bone, and snort, "Mind if I take it back and get it in my *real* size?"

A man, much like a mentally deficient person, excels in playing repetitive, simplistic games with his dog.

Here are some games that he (and his dog) seem to like:

• The man throws a rock on the ground. The dog picks it up. The man throws a rock on the ground. The dog picks it up. The man throws a rock on the ground. The dog barks and picks it up.

• The man tries to take a rag out of the dog's mouth. The dog does not let go of the rag. The dog makes guttural, choking noises. The man laughs.

• The man puts tape on the dog's nose. The dog runs around the room, trying to take the tape off. The man laughs.

In return for all this, a man's dog gives him complete unquestioning devotion; and good gosh, who wouldn't?

IN SUMMARY

Never try to come between a man and his dog. (Especially since you can't tell whether that winsome little pooch has had *attack training*.)

But do beware if your man offers to walk the dog *very* frequently in the warmer months. Men who walk the dog frequently in the warmer months are looking for Bad Women.

Cats

Men do not like cats, because cats are smarter than they are. (Cats are smarter than *you* are, too, but you can live with it.)

A man does not trust cats, because cats do not understand revered American concepts like the Work Ethic, the Nuclear Family, and Red Meat. (Nowadays, cats don't even eat "cat food." They eat things with French names that come in expensive foil pouches and smell better than what people eat. Mackerel *a la moutarde*.)

What's the matter with red meat, a guy says. Meat is good enough for dogs, a guy says. Cats are sissies. Cats should have that smug look wiped off their faces.

When you are not around, your man has all sorts of unseemly dialogues with your cat. Maybe you should spy on him sometime. These are some of the things he says:

- "Hell-o, Bootsie. We're looking *self-satisfied* today, aren't we?"
- "And what are our plans for this afternoon, Bootsie? How about if we just *sit* there for about three hours. Wouldn't that be nice? To just *sit* there and digest a whole two-pound bag of Little Friskies and contribute absolute *zippo* to the human race?"
- "How would you like to go for a little *swim* in the sump pump, Bootsie?"

When you are around, your man enjoys playing amusing *games* with your cat. Here are some of them:

- Putting the cat's head in his mouth, to make you scream.
- Holding the cat upside down, so you can see the whites of its eyes.

• Launching the cat aloft with a small, Forward-Passing motion; trying to make the cat land on its back.

What you must do is not *react* when your man tries these tactics. He is simply acting on his deep-seated hostilities, and your cat can handle this with more sangfroid than you can.

SPECIAL OCCASIONS

Holidays

You knew your relationship had really sprouted roots the year you first had to decide whose parents you were going to spend Christmas with. Most "real" couples spend their holidays on one of America's lovely INTERSTATE HIGHWAYS, practicing a unique kind of holiday shuttle diplomacy.

They know that *someone's* parents are never going to speak to them again if they don't at least "put in an appearance" at *all* the holiday family gatherings to which they are invited. But you will have to accept that—*you are never going to make everybody happy* for Christmas or Easter or the annual Fourth of July picnic, where Uncle Jimmy (who's "not getting any younger, but *please don't feel guilty*") is going to do his special imitations of the Andrews Sisters and Elmer Fudd.

The best you can do is wait for the day when humans can *beam* themselves to Metuchen, New Jersey, just like in *Star Trek*. Maybe it'll happen in your grandchildren's lifetime. Assuming they ever want to visit you.

Birthday: Yours

No one knows where the expression "Happy Birthday" originates, since it implies that the mass recognition of one's inexorable aging (and physical decline) should inspire in one a joyful, positive reaction.

It rarely inspires this reaction in women. Some women look at birthdays as a celebration simply of making it through another year. (Of work, play, boring dinner parties, menstruation, yet another "Battle of the Network Stars," and mass purchases of pet food.)

You should consider yourself lucky if your man makes a a big deal of your birthday. It is a myth that most men forget women's birthdays. What they actually do is sublimate the *sentiment* that birthdays inspire, and they walk around *appearing* not to remember your birthday. Sometimes this *appearance* can continue for several years in a row.

The question is, do you really want to make a big, operatic deal about this issue? If you really want to nail your guy, there are better days to do it.

Birthday: His

The salient question about men's birthdays is: Even though he *says* he doesn't, DOES HE WANT YOU TO SURPRISE HIM?

Let's examine surprise parties for a minute: They always make you look awfully good, don't they? You get to buzz about the house in a cute hostess gown, placating the guests before he arrives, saying, "Do you think he *knows*? Do you think he *suspects*? I'm going to *die*. I'm so *nervous*." Guests can be very impressed by this sort of thing.

But what makes you think that when the moment of moments arrives, and he opens the door to all those pink, beaming faces, and they all yell You Know What at him, he is going to be overcome with joy?

Why would a man who breaks out in hives if you give him Bran *Chex* in the morning instead of Bran *Buds*—why would this self-same man enjoy the experience of walking into his private space one evening, dog tired after a day at the office, and seeing forty-five people dressed like Ringling Brothers rejects screaming "For He's a Jolly Good Fellow" at him, when in fact he is neither

• jolly, nor
• good, nor

- in any mood for fellowship, especially since he's already noticed the spot your friend's husband, Chester, left on the upholstery with his cigar.

This is one of the great mysteries of Western civilization. They do not have surprise birthday parties in Japan.

Anniversaries

If you are legally married, you get to celebrate your pledge of eternal love year after year with thoughtful gifts of silver, gold, aluminum, bronze, paper, and other mysterious modern alloys. These gifts ensure that, as a pair, you are Worth Something. Your relationship has a certain heft (and clank) to it.

One of the difficulties of not being married is that you don't really have an anniversary to celebrate. (And you get exactly goose egg in the gift department.) But very resourceful couples usually come up with some date or another to circle on their pocket calendars and get misty-eyed over, and here are some of my favorite suggestions.

ANNIVERSARY OF MEETING IN THE OFFICE

If you worked in the same office, you probably remember the moment your eyes met across the teased head of the fat lady with the sandwich cart. And He said something like, "I'll have an egg salad sandwich and a V-8."

And you tried to keep your love a secret from everyone. You passed funny notes in interoffice envelopes. You arrived at work on separate buses. You were crazy, impetuous fools—you met with coffee and hoagies in the office parking garage, and said, "Someday we won't have to hide. . . . We'll go above ground." And you eventually did, to Pizza Hut, and eventually everyone knew you were an Item, and you didn't care anymore.

Those were the days.

ANNIVERSARY OF YOUR FIRST DATE

Let's put it this way: He probably did not bring you a corsage, meet your parents, or bring you home by ten.

He probably bought you some Mateus rosé, met your cat, and jumped on your bones sometime after midnight; but you thought he was sort of cute, so you said, "Why not? I'm a grown-up. And he closely resembles one. . . ."

Can you remember that long ago? Can you remember what you had for dinner? You found part of a ventilation hose in your hamburger, and you both laughed about it. He said, "I'll complain to the manager," and you said, "No, don't bother. It would destroy the moment." But you liked the idea of his being your hamburger savior, your all-beef-patty knight in shining armor.

After dinner, he explained the deep subtext of some Simon and Garfunkel lyrics to you, and you thought to yourself, "I could definitely remove my L'eggs for this guy."

And that's how it all began. Memories are made of this.

ANNIVERSARY OF YOUR FIRST FIGHT

Many couples feel their relationship has never really reached Cruising Velocity until they've had their first knockdown, drag-out brawl. And when you're living together, that memorable occasion has a special poignancy.

Remember the first time you walked out of the house, swearing you were never coming back? It took a while for the important questions to finally filter into your brain: "WHY AM I DOING THIS?" and then, "WHERE THE HELL AM I GOING TO GO?" (No normal person ever lives at the same zip code as her parents anymore, so that option is usually out of the question. And you're afraid your friends will think you're a meringue brain for wandering around town in the middle of the night.)

So you spent three hours at a place called Dizzy's Hide-a-way drinking decaffeinated coffee and listening to some bricklayer complaining about how the phone company is owned by the Communist party, and then used your last dime to call him back, saying, "I'm not really coming back to *you*, okay? I just need a place to spend the night. *But this doesn't mean anything.*"

Eventually, of course, you had sex and made up. So here's to you, you two romantic so-and-sos.

Stepping Out

If he "never takes you anywhere," it could be for one of two reasons: He's a stiff. Or he is sick and tired of enduring a certain ritual that men have put up with for centuries. And, we are bound to admit, with an admirable lack of complaint: Men and women always take different amounts of time to leave the house. "Ready" means different things to men and women. "Ready," for a man, means standing at the door, cowlick corrected, car keys in hand.

"Ready," for a woman, is not a fixed point in time, but rather an extended period in time. It is rather like time-lapse photography of a germinating plant.

A woman must necessarily go through the phases of Pre-Ready (dressed, looking for pearl stud earrings), Sub-Ready (still dressed, including shoes, still looking for pearl stud earrings), Quasi-Ready (still dressed, different shoes, gold belt that doesn't match pearl stud earrings; now looking for gold earrings), Pre-Finally Ready (now changing dress, which doesn't go with either gold belt or gold earrings; also, hair must be completely rearranged), and Ultimately Ready (happy with dress; can't find curling iron, however).

Man makes all kinds of threats, veiled and unveiled, at such times. He has worn a little hole in the carpet in front of the door, and there is a little gray stain on the ceiling from where he's been playing catch with the keys.

"I'm leaving *now*," he says.

"Yeah," you shout from upstairs. "I'm ready. I'm really, really ready."

"I mean it," he says. He doesn't raise his voice. He says this in a very monotonous tone, like a Gregorian chant. "I'm really, really leaving."

"Yeah, yeah," you say from upstairs. "Okay, I'm coming right now."

"I'm starting the car," he says. "You *hear* that the car is starting. I'm leaving without you."

"O-*kay*," you say. (You're deciding you can put on the red lacquer earrings in the car. As soon as you find them.)

When you finally make it downstairs, he is more than a

little put out and talks to you out of the back of his head. "We're going to be late," he says. "They said seven-thirty."

"Yeah, yeah," you say. "I was ready. I was really ready."

In all, we are talking about a total of fifteen to twenty minutes, during all of which time you were "ready" but not ULTRA-READY. This is the mistake most couples make—a simple one of semantics. You could set him straight on this issue very easily, but you are always living with the fear that if you confess to a need for ten more minutes, in order to attain ULTRA-READINESS (or, U minus ten) that HE REALLY WILL LEAVE YOU BEHIND.

But ask yourself what the odds are of this actually happening: Men don't really like driving around alone all night, just to prove a point. And showing up at a dinner party without you requires a highly creative explanation. Most of all, remember that men really do like being unable to understand certain things about your modus operandi.

It gives human biology a certain *piquance*. (This is too subtle a concept for men to understand.)

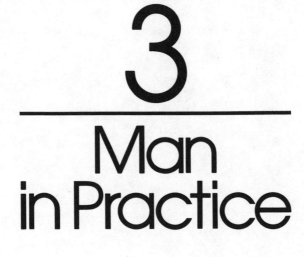

3

Man
in Practice

THE WIELDING OF POWER

NOWADAYS when a stranger calls and says, "May I speak to the head of the household?" do you know what to say?

If you haven't held a coronation lately, there probably is no real "head." But whoever lets the ice cube trays go the longest without ever refilling them, that is the person in POWER.

You may dislike hearing the word "power" used in reference to the intimate, tender relationship that you and your man undoubtedly share.

But I've heard worse. I've heard living together referred to as out-and-out *war*. Why else do people use phrases like, "What do you want—a *medal*?" whenever they feel as if they're losing valuable territory. No one ever says, *"Yes, I want a medal"* (although it would be an interesting approach). No one has ever actually awarded herself (or himself) a Purple Heart, or a *Legion d'Honneur,* just for walking the dog or sitting through another horrible evening of Gene Pitney records. . . .

But the *politics* of living together are always out there somewhere, throwing a little curve into everything you do. And I'm going to drag sex into this now, because other experts do, and they seem to get away with it.

Take this little QUIZ for a minute.

I would use sex to get
a) out of my parents' house
b) just about anything

c) a Ginsu knife

d) a pat on the head afterward.

You see, it is just a myth that men are always trying to get women into bed. Once you and your man are living together, you will probably try to get *him* into bed, at least once in your career, just to get his attention.

You are probably not the only person who has ever done this, so don't feel too cheesy about it. There's a principle at work here: Men control the reins of power in most other areas of life, and bed is the one place where women almost always feel power—once you've got him glued to you like a postage stamp, if he's not in your power now, he never will be.

Now here's the moral issue: Should you knowingly use these moments to talk men into things? If you've read your history, you know that women like Madame du Barry always waited for life's breathless little instants to order a new tiara, or a wig stand, or a coach-and-four, or something. And you know that there is a word for women who do things like this.

Now about that quiz.

If you answered that "I would use sex to get out of my parents' house," you are like almost every woman who got married before 1968.

If you answered "I would use sex to get just about anything," at least you have no romantic illusions that will have to be dispelled.

If you answered "I would use sex to get a Ginsu knife," you also have no romantic illusions, but you are completely tacky. (What are they, $9.95 or something?)

If you answered "I would use sex to get a pat on the head afterward," you are pretty much in the mainstream of American women.

This is a sad commentary on the state of human sexual relations. But you should know that intimacy is tough, sweaty, dirt-under-the-fingernails *work*. This part of the book will help you know whether you're putting in enough woman-hours, and whether you're using them to best advantage.

STUPID VOICES IN OUR TIME

MANY women say, "My man and I have not yet reached the stage in our relationship where we can converse with each other in stupid voices. And yet, is this phenomenon not the hallmark of a successful, close relationship?"

Of course it is. Baby talk, high-pitched squeaks, and spontaneous imitations of Alvin and the Chipmunks—True Intimacy is founded on these building blocks. No one knows at what point each couple finds its unique repertoire of Stupid Voices to utilize, but when the time comes, you will both know it.

Most of us only use our Stupid Voices in private. In bed, on the telephone, while waiting in the car at the drive-in teller.

But STUPID VOICES ARE NOTHING TO BE ASHAMED OF.

History now knows that many noted public figures have conversed with their loved ones in this manner. President and Mrs. ZACHARY TAYLOR and the Roman emperor CAESAR AGRIPPA and his empress have been among them.

There is even evidence that Supreme Court Justice SANDRA DAY O'CONNOR converses in a stupid voice with her husband. When she is in chambers and she receives a call from MR. O'CONNOR, her voice becomes very high and she calls her husband "Pookie."

ORAL SEX

THERE was a time when oral sex was not a prerequisite for being asked to live with a man. There were women on the outside who were *paid* to do this. It was sort of like having your shirts sent out. Thirty years ago, your mother had to waste a lot of time looking for lipstick on your dad's collar *and* on his boxer shorts.

But now, with the popularization of works like *3-D Vixen Babysitters* on cable, men can shop around for their sexual *divertissements,* and many have come to the conclusion, "Hey, I want that. And under my own roof."

And yet, the quality of oral sex in our country has reached a deplorable state. Surveys show that the majority of college graduates talk far too much while performing it. And though it can be effectively argued that, if women were biologically meant to perform oral sex on men, they would have been born without teeth, many men feel that this is really no excuse for a lot of slacking off on the job.

I won't lie to you and say that quality matters more than quantity. Even if you like to perform it eleven times a day, he will still spend a lot of time hunched in his favorite comfy chair, wondering where all the magic has gone from your relationship.

Bear in mind: EVERYTHING IN LIFE REMINDS HIM OF ORAL SEX. Watching you eat a chili dog reminds him of oral sex. Jacuzzis remind him of oral sex. Trout fishing reminds him of oral sex. Trying to distract him does not work.

Therefore, it is very important for the two of you to keep the ORAL SEX LINES OF COMMUNICATION open. Explain to him that these are some examples of the WRONG way of going about getting it:

- "Hey, Grace, I want some *oral sex,* and pronto."
- "*I've* got an idea—how's about dinner, a show, and then some *oral sex.*"
- "Remember last summer down at the lake? The hypnotic moonlight? The whispering pines? The *oral sex?*"

Actually, the average man is very unforthcoming about making his desires known. Frequently, he says nothing at all. Here are some ways to know he wants It:

- He arrives at more than one meal wearing no pants.
- He spends a lot of time hanging from his chin-up bar so that you cannot enter the breakfast nook without passing your head between his inseams.
- He feeds the pets while wearing no pants.

A lot of us walk around thinking, "There are things that everyone but me knows about oral sex."

This is probably true.

Are these things learnable from books? In a society that has provided the needy with tennis clinics and computer golf therapy, why are there no remedial oral-sex training programs? Unless you have grown up in France or somewhere, it is not a skill that is taught and discussed intelligently at family meals.

Claiming that you are a Buddhist does not let you off the hook for long. Nor does being a vegetarian, painfully shy, a picky eater, or a member of the Republican party.

If the idea doesn't fill you with feverish delight, men feel that the first thing you'll need to work on is your attitude. Some women ask, since it is volunteer work, whether it is tax deductible. I tell them, *"Let's be adults here."* If you do not love it after the first 480 or so tries, maybe you are playing the wrong musical selections. Try something with more woodwinds. Try some Mahler—he can be quite "inconclusive." Try some middle-period Roy Orbison.

Some women wonder whether it is okay to back out once one has started. It is absolutely not okay. *This is not like faking cramps to get out of phys. ed., okay? This is real life.* Do you know what happens if you turn off a dishwasher or a washing machine during the rinse cycle? Some things in nature have a distinct beginning, middle, and end. Interrupting a man's *natural sequence* can cause embolism, pulmonary thrombosis, or other permanent physical damage.

Or this is what men tell you. No one knows where they get all their information on this subject, but it certainly seems to be extensive.

MOMENTS OF EXQUISITE CRISIS: OLD GIRLFRIENDS

THIS is how you will find out about the old girlfriend he never got over: He will be showing you slides of his trip to Gran Canaria three years ago, and suddenly there will be a shot of a nymph with flaxen curls, a smile like the Fourth of July, and legs that could make grown men lie down in front of bulldozers.

"Oops," he will say. "How did *that* get in there?"

That got in there because he bloody well wanted it to get in there.

Former girlfriends always have names like Randee and Candee and Sandee, and they are almost always flight attendants. ("Well, she was actually a member of MENSA," he will tell you. "She wasn't really *into* serving moistened towelettes to people.")

Men get very jovial and "positive" when they try to introduce you to the Idea of old girlfriends. They enjoy detailing the *many* things the two of you have in common.

But you have eyes in your head, don't you? Old girlfriends have a way of leaving unpleasant relics around your man's house, and you have viewed these items close up: Snoopy shower curtains. Cute, heart-shaped picture frames. His 'n' hers cup hooks. The sight of these things may cause you to shake noticeably with revulsion, but DO NOT PASS VALUE JUDGMENTS UPON THEM IN THE PRESENCE OF YOUR GUY. He will get a peculiarly coy, vacant look on his face in the presence of these artifacts. It will remind you of the look he had when the two of you went to his hometown, and he visited his Little League pitching mound.

Men don't change. Just their taste in mounds.

If a breakup is of recent vintage, a man may feel that you will be "threatened" by his old girlfriend. So he just sort of forgets to tell you about her. And, coincidentally, he just sort of forgets to tell her about *you*. And, naturally, someday the phone is going to ring when he's out. And you will answer it and a tender little voice will say:

"Who are YOU?"

And in your shock and confusion, you will manage to say something like, "I'm just here to clean up." (Not even a lie in most cases.)

And then one of three things will happen:

- If she's not very nice to you, you are in an extremely good position. Obviously she wants him back, so he can't be the unredeemed drip you thought he was an hour ago.
- If she *is* nice to you, she is definitely psychotic, and she is on her way over to cut off your private parts with a steak knife.
- If she is very, very nice to you, it is because she has just joined a religious cult, and she is on her way over to sell you some rose water.

In most of these instances, it is never quite clear who broke up with whom. (Your man, when he returns, will be slightly put out that you answered the phone *just because it was ringing*. And then the two of you will have a Meaningful Dialogue about his past, and your place in his future.)

Why do old girlfriends, not to mention ex-wives, bother you so much?

Why does Soviet first-strike capability bother you so much? There are a lot of *abstractions* in life that are just horrible enough to keep you from sleeping nights.

The worst thing you can find out about an old girlfriend is that she "had a few problems in her life." This is *never* a good sign for you: She was an epileptic, say, who went on to become a news anchorwoman and adopt a family of Lebanese refugees. (She was a saint. You will never measure up.) Either that, or she was a pill freak who also used to date George Hamilton and Prince Albert of Monaco, and once refused to get out of bed because she thought her apartment was revolving like the Seattle Space Needle. She will call from Barcelona, at four in the morning, needing money.

Your man will assure you that because of all her problems, this woman "never liked sex as much as you do." (But he will manage to let you know she always seemed to be around to give him limitless quantities of it.)

Very often, this old flame has "tragic problems with her *family*." But she, saint that she was, never let it get in the way of being impish and perky. Also, these problems, terrible as they were, always made her *not want to eat*.

Your problems always make you want to eat, but *she* always had the kind of problems that made her *thin*. She had so many problems, she could have modeled in a Sears catalogue. *Underwear* even.

If you are very, very lucky, you will never meet this person. But you won't be that lucky. There will probably be some kind of "social occasion" where the two of you will end up nose to nose—or, worse, he will get the idea that it would be really keen for the two of you to "get acquainted."

And there she'll be, and there you'll be, and there he'll be, and if you say *anything* to her like, "I've heard so much about you," she will know you for the unregenerate coward you are.

As you talk to her, look out for the following WARNING SIGNS:

- Are you smiling like Miss Kansas or someone with lockjaw when no one is saying anything funny?
- Is she referring to him as "Gumby," while you are referring to him as "Mr. Reynolds?"
- Do you keep smoothing out wrinkles in your dress when you're wearing shorts?
- When you say, "We must do this again sometime," do you sound as sincere as a Universal Studios tour guide?

The funny thing about all this is, despite all your most valiant efforts, you will realize in the long run that you can never truly *hate* this woman. She just *knows* too much. About him. You end up being impressed by the fact that she too has heard him trying to sound like Julius La Rosa in the shower; and she didn't walk out on him on the spot, either.

One thing you must manage never to do is ask a man a question like, "Did you love her more than you love me?" (You must never ask him this, but you will find some way to worm the information out of him.) He'll probably say something like, "You can't make comparisons."

Pepsi and Coke can make comparisons. It's part of the American way. But you will find that as soon as he starts talking about you and his old girlfriend, he will start sounding like some kind of foreigner:

"It was a very special experience with Monica and me," he will say. "But now it's just a beautiful little part of my memory."

Who the hell actually talks like that in real life? And you shudder a little bit to think that one day he could be saying these things about *you*.

OLD BOYFRIENDS

THE main point in having boyfriends is so that they can evolve to the point of being *old* boyfriends.

An old boyfriend can be vastly preferable to a current one, because you invariably forget that he used to wear V-neck undershirts and say things like "Down the hatch!" at formal dinner parties.

You must remember that he was perfect:
- He was the only guy who ever brought you tulips.
- He was the guy who could make your mother laugh at really awful knock-knock jokes.

- He was the guy who held your head on the night you discovered you'd never be able to drink Scotch on a recreational basis.

And admit it: This guy Chet, or whoever he is, is the Sword of Damocles you hold over your current guy's head. When you say things like, "Next to my *father*, Chet was the only guy who . . ." you don't really think you're making a "casual remark," do you?

You don't have to invoke the *name* of your O.B., either, for his presence to be felt. All you have to do is drive past the restaurant where the two of you used to listen to Danny and the Juniors records, and sigh meaningfully. You could mention leather fashions and motorcycle boots with spurs in a menacingly approving way. You could say, "Sometimes I wonder if *anything* will ever be like 1965 again." (A ridiculous thing to say: 1965, by overwhelming world consensus, ought to have been canceled entirely. This is why it is such an effective tactic.)

Incidents with Old Boyfriends always have names like New Wave European movies:
- "That Summer in Sandusky"
- "Those Breathless Years with Mac"
- "That Sultry Evening at Jack in the Box"
- "Wild Weekend at University of Connecticut Department of Psychology"

Maybe you even have fantasies about being fought over by your O.B. and your present guy. Maybe you think that the two of them *put together* would make the perfect man. But in fact, by this point in your life, you've actually *made up* sterling qualities in your old boyfriend that never even existed. This is called "the halo effect." (Because everyone's old boyfriend is sort of like Jesus: You can always resurrect him when you need him.)

You never know for sure when your present guy is actively jealous of the Man from Your Past. Sometimes, when the subject has come up rather often, he'll just start acting darned peculiar. He might eat fourteen packages of licorice whips, then go for a long walk in a hailstorm. He might spend the morning reading his old collection of Spider Man comics, with a horrible kind of concentration.

You can always *ask* if he is jealous. He will make a noise as if a large toad is lodged in his throat, which in some languages means "yes."

But you have to realize that men are different from women in this particular area. Your guy doesn't really care about the walks in the moonlight you took with this joker; or about the marriage proposal you received in relish letters on a cheeseburger; or about how much the two of you enjoyed that fruity movie remake of *Romeo and Juliet* with the nude scene.

Your guy is concerned about *stats,* about *numbers,* about *hard* (yes, I know what I'm saying here) *facts.*

After a long silence, he may bring this up just as you are drifting off to sleep:

Him: "Well, it probably wasn't that big a deal. Right?"

You: "I don't know. The usual size. I'm going to sleep now."

Him: "What's 'usual'? How 'usual'? 'Usual' as in Lincoln Logs?"

This is why it is okay to make qualitative, but never *quantitative* comparisons between your men. The occasional, casually cruel remark about being swept off your feet by some past Mr. Wonderful never hurt anybody.

But never bring statistics, measurements, and League Standings into this. You could do lifelong damage.

HIS MOTHER

EVERY man has two significant parents.

They are both his mother. A man's mother has had twice as much influence on his behavior as any other human, living or dead.

A man's mother is his personal archivist, and his window on the past. She has kept his room in better shape than the

Smithsonian has kept the personal library of Ulysses S. Grant. She always hated the medal he got for holding his breath the longest at Camp Woodchuck, but she'd never throw it away. She is still getting half of his junk mail from God knows where, and she guards it zealously with her life. She will never understand why you are systematically starving her son to death.

A man's mother is the only person who really knows how to communicate with him, who knows his private quirks and queer habits, his likes and dislikes. SHE ALONE KNOWS WHY HE HATES BAKED HAM.

SHE ALONE ENJOYS PREPARING BAKED HAM FOR HIM (although she knows he hates it) BECAUSE SHE ENJOYS FIGHTING WITH HIM ABOUT IT IN A WAY YOU'LL NEVER TRULY UNDERSTAND.

> *Him:* "I don't understand why you made me this. You know I hate it."
>
> *His Mother:* "What do you mean? You don't hate it."
>
> *Him:* "I hate it. I hated it when we lived in the old house, too."
>
> *His Mother:* "You did not hate it when we lived in the old house."
>
> *Him:* "What difference does it make? *I hate it now.*"
>
> *His Mother:* "Why? Why do you hate it?"
>
> (Had enough? They haven't.)
>
> *Him:* "Because I just do. I don't know. I hate it. It's *pink.*"
>
> *His Mother:* "Oh, great. That's just great."

You have to realize that these conversations serve a very useful function. Without them, your man would feel unmoored, adrift. Somehow, a baked ham connects him with the vanished utopia of his youth.

Meeting a man's mother for the first time is naturally going to be a very traumatic experience for you. (His father is never a problem. His father is happy he's going out with anyone at all, because it means he isn't gay.) She may not like your religion; she may not like your hair color. You may have to brace yourself to change both of them. There's no getting around this principle: When you figure out what it is a man's mother wants from you, GIVE IT TO HER. Do you want him to have to choose between her and you? Do you have to be told what his selection is going to be? This is a woman who even loves the *disgusting* things about him. Do you think he's going to waste a *minute* in the decision-making process?

When you meet a man's mother, she will never be overtly rude to you; which will probably throw you off your guard for a little while.

But remember: On first meeting, a man's mother *never* asks you "innocuous" questions. You have to be prepared to *translate* the things she is saying to you.

Here are some examples.

"Do you work, Dear?"	"Are you sterile?"
"Where do you buy your meatballs? Or do you make your own?"	"You don't cook. That's pretty obvious."
"Where do you come from originally?"	"You're going to make him leave town, aren't you? You're going to stick a knife in my heart, aren't you?"
"I like your dress."	"I'm surprised he let you wear that dress, when he knows *I* wouldn't wear that dress."

Once you get down these simple principles of vocabulary, I shouldn't think you'll have too many problems with Mom in the future.

But you should know that certain subjects will never be safe. There are only about three or four hundred subjects that you have to worry about. Memorize them, and *think fast* when they crop up "by accident":

THESE SUBJECTS ARE USUALLY SAFE TO TALK ABOUT:
- pets and pet products
- car maintenance
- the weather (not the *seasons*—that can lead to HOLIDAYS. Avoid HOLIDAYS.)
- current movies (not *films*)

- bridge
- coffee making (not *food*. Never food.)
- *your* mother
- bargello

YOU SHOULD ABSOLUTELY NEVER TALK TO A MAN'S MOTHER ABOUT:

- his father
- fashion
- children
- current events
- your future
- your past
- any disease
- convenience laundry products

It is very silly for you to be *afraid* of a man's mother. She has only had him for twenty years or so. Whereas your contract with him has an option for renewal, and on an indefinite basis.

And she is very aware of this. She is the one, you see, who is afraid of *you*. You go bump in the night. *With her little guy.* That's a hard one for her.

So practice a little charity.

YOUR MOTHER

MEN used to say to each other, "If you ever want to know exactly how your future wife is going to turn out, just take a good look at her mother."

This is true.

Your mind, to a man, is like a lost civilization with a language all its own. Introducing him to your mother is like giving him a Rosetta stone.

For this reason, I don't think you should ever introduce a man to your mother.

But if you *do* introduce him to your mother, you should never upon *never* leave him *alone* with her.

Such actions have a history of tragic consequences. In the days when power car windows were first being invented, women over fifty were incapable of operating them. It was possible to lock middle-aged women in Pontiacs at the Safeway, where under certain temperatures they would fry to a golden brown, much to the amusement of their sons-in-law.

This practice is now less fashionable. But why push it?

"VENGEANCE IS MINE," SAYETH THE LORD. "WHETHER *YOU* SHOULD MESS WITH IT IS ANOTHER STORY."

MANY of us dream about exacting our revenge for offenses —real and imagined—committed in the home: criminally negligent soiling of kitchen surfaces, infidelities (both first and second degree), Grumpiness. Dopiness, Sneeziness, Sleaziness . . .

Thankfully, few of us act on our dreams of revenge. Most of us have very unrealistic pictures of what revenge really *is*. We think of it as a point of Finality. The End of the Road. We expect it to be *understood* as a comeuppance. We expect our guy to say something along the lines of: "Wow, touché, honey. I guess I won't do *that* again."

NO MAN HAS EVER SAID THESE WORDS.

There is no such thing as Ultimate Revenge. Even if you

"really put a person in his place," there is no possibility whatever THAT HE WILL WANT TO STAY THERE. If you've really got him in a corner, he's going to hear the bell and come out with his dukes up.

He will try to take his revenge on you.

And then you will avenge his revenge.

This is very sick. It is one of the cornerstones of American family life. It is called the ETERNAL REVENGE PRINCIPLE.

And it almost always leads to:

Arguing.

In the same way that many of us misunderstand the fundamentals of *vengeance,* most of us *completely* misunderstand the fundamentals of *arguing.*

We mistakenly feel that the point of arguing is to WIN. And it's not. The point of ARGUING is to ARGUE.

It is a bad idea to be a *habitual* winner of arguments: A "WINNABLE" HOME ARGUMENT IS LIKE A "WINNABLE" NUCLEAR WAR—WHEN IT'S ALL OVER, LIFE AS YOU KNOW IT WILL NOT BE WORTH LIVING.

If you get known around the community as a winner of arguments, doors will be shut to you; welcome mats will be rescinded. "Call in the dogs, Martha," the neighbors will say. "She WINS TOO MANY ARGUMENTS."

Losing an argument is a noble art. Your guy will probably end up saying to you, "Oh, *that's* okay, honey." And then he will ask you to have sex with him.

(A lot of men do find it erotic to see you all hopped up about something. They have already decided you can't possibly have a point, but they like to see you spitting fire and venom, and hyperventilating, and so on. Perhaps you remember the movie *Duel in the Sun* with Gregory Peck and Jennifer Jones—they shot each other to death before their last kiss, but if they had been rushed to the emergency room and had their lives restored, the sex would have been *great.*)

You are maybe not impressed by what I have said so far. You are maybe convinced that there is *some* form of honorable expression of differences, which will get you what you want out of your man.

You think you're some kind of intelligent piece of work, don't you? You think you're a pretty *controlled* kind of person, don't you, or you wouldn't be disputing what you're reading here.

But let me tell you something, Miss Smarty-Pants: People are never dignified when they're fighting. People are never in control.

Fights are exactly like horror movies.

You know the scene where there's a dark, creepy house, and you are mentally screaming to the heroine, "Don't go in the house. *Don't go in the house.*" She always goes in the house.

Well, sometimes when you are fighting with your man, you will be mentally screaming to yourself, "Don't bring up his friend Louie again. *Don't bring up his friend Louie again.*" But you always bring up Louie again. You can't help it. The only difference between your domestic quarrels and Hitchcock is that with Hitchcock you get to finish your Milk Duds and go home. (And there is probably nothing in Hitchcock as truly repellent as his friend Louie.)

ADVANCED ARGUING: PSYCHOLOGY IN THE HOME

IF you have ever taken Introductory Psychology in college, I'm sure you feel you are well qualified to analyze most of your mate's behavior—providing "resonance" for all the mysterious actions that even *he* might not understand.

Even if you do not have a firm grip on the *principles* of psychology, you do have at your disposal an impressive battery of psychological *terms,* which you can pull out of a hat at will.

Let's take the concept of "projection," which in America unfortunately does not take place in movie theaters alone. In "projection," a man takes a quality he dislikes in himself and *projects* it on you.

"You are so indecisive," he may say.

"How do you mean that?" you may say. "How am I indecisive?"

"Well, I could mean it any number of ways," he may say.

"Aha!" you say. "Projection!"

Many women do that. They shout out one-word analyses of human behavior in stentorian tones, then sit around and wait for applause for their insights.

Do you think life is some kind of *bingo* game? "Projection!" "Hostility!" "Inadequacy!"

If Parker Brothers thought these were proper themes for games, they would have copyrighted these expressions by now. Did your father like it when your mother did this? Or did he buy himself a train set and lock himself in the basement and pretend not to understand English?

Women have a habit of accusing men of things they are logically unable to disprove. Take misogyny: the current theory that all men, deep down in their horrid little hearts, SECRETLY HATE AND FEAR WOMEN.

There is no way that a man can prove to you empirically that he doesn't hate women. Sometimes, as a negotiating tool, he will confess to you that he does hate *selected* women. (He knows that hating your mother, for example, is not the same as hating *all* women. Your mother has been working on certain irritating qualities all her life, whereas most other women are rank amateurs.)

There is only one area in your shared life with a man in which arguing is a regular and constant necessity:

HOW TO FIGHT ABOUT MONEY

Too many amateurs attempt to stage serious financial altercations and get hurt. But it's one of the few important things in your relationship you can't hire someone else to do.

You probably watched your parents fight about money (they wouldn't have wanted you to pick up this sort of thing on the *street*), so you probably know a lot of the ground rules. No one is ever wrong, and no one is ever right. Everyone is just *loud*.

Money is what causes wrinkles. (Little kids don't have money, do they? And they don't have wrinkles.) Even if you split everything fifty-fifty, as they tell you to do in all the chic magazines, *someone's* fifty always looks more like sixty-five and up.

And men will always do things with their money that you can't understand. They will gamble it on Oilers games, for fun. And you think that this makes about as much sense as sticking your head in a pencil sharpener, for fun.

Ground Rules

I always recommend that couples should have their first big fight about money in front of guests. Your friends always tend to doubt the seriousness of your commitment until they hear you talking (or, better yet, screaming) dollars and cents. It can start out with just a well-placed little jab:

"*Bruce* here bought this really *high-quality vodka* we're drinking here tonight. I guess he thought Catherine the Great was coming to dinner. *With her horse.*"

"Susan here thought we needed curtains just like the ones

she saw in the April *Casa Vogue*. Personally, my taste is a little more *heterosexual* than that."

Also, for good measure, bring up his parents a lot:

"I'm sorry, Geoffrey. I didn't spend my summers on *Block Island*. I didn't go to *Choate*. My father wasn't a *lackey* for *Union Carbide*. I am *sorry*."

When people fight about money, they always say, "I am *sorry*."

They're not sorry. It's just part of the grammar of fights —it takes up necessary space, like the slow movement of a violin concerto. "Excuse *me*," is another thing they say— when they're being inexcusable.

Money fights are usually completely confusing to the participants involved. What most people don't understand is that we have *all* had a "deprived childhood." We all carry around, clutched fiercely to our breasts, the belief that *our* childhood was more *resoundingly* deprived than the next person's. It gives life a bittersweet quality.

Much as in Scarlett O'Hara's famous "I'll never go hungry again" speech, many women walk around saying to themselves, "When I have two quarters to rub together, I know what I'm going to do."

And you know something? Whatever it is, it will never (and this is a serious NEVER) be what your man wants to do.

Maybe you say, "I will never wear two pairs of panty-hose at the same time because both pairs have run up one leg, and I can't afford $2.50 for a *new* pair."

Whereas *he* says, "I will never again drive a Japanese fuel-efficient automobile, or a K car, when I can drive a Maserati."

So you've got problems, haven't you? These tragic discrepancies in life aspirations go way, way back in human history. There is an inscription on an Egyptian tomb in Thebes showing a supplicating woman saying, "You have squandered twelve pieces of silver on a camel then, Nonesh? Terrific. Just terrific."

It is important to distinguish between mere "money conflict" and the inexorable knowledge that you're in *serious* trouble.

The time to start worrying is when he says, "I don't want you to worry about money."

Every working man deserves a mate like June Allyson in *The Glenn Miller Story*. She kept her household afloat by regularly stealing money from Jimmy Stewart's wallet, and opening a bank account with it. And even though she inwardly believed that musicians were degenerates and no-accounts, she stood by him, always knowing he would someday write "Moonlight Serenade," without which the Germans would have won World War II.

If you pulled this kind of stunt nowadays, you'd get a lot of abuse; and frankly I think you'd deserve it. You should let a man worry about his money, and you should worry about yours.

If you don't have any money, get some.

If you have money, you have to decide whether there is any *advantage* to the two of you pooling your resources.

Remember: THERE IS NO LAW THAT SAYS YOU HAVE TO DO THIS. Fortunately, the days are gone when a man, just by living with you, had the right to sell your private property, your jewels, your Matisses, and your coffee plantation in Jamaica.

Here is a good way of figuring out a JOINT BUDGET:
1. Write down how much money you make.
2. Write down how much money he makes.
3. Write down how much money he thinks he will make when he really makes a "name" for himself.
4. Write down how much money you will make after you have taken assertiveness training, a few drinks, and est.
5. Subtract 1 from 4. That is your *expectation variable*.
6. Is his expectation variable (subtract 2 from 3) higher than yours? A lot higher? Is it in fact the most laughable piece of optimism you've heard in a dog's age?
7. Tell him to keep his money to himself.

SEXUAL PROBLEMS

I met a very modern kind of guy recently. An articulate, unthreatened, sensitive-talking guy (the kind of guy who could insouciantly model cable-knit sweaters and casual, nipped-waist jackets in *Esquire*), and I said to this person, "Where do you think all the romance has gone from modern life? Why do romance-minded women so often seem to get (as social commentator Marilyn Monroe put it) 'The fuzzy end of the lollipop'?"

And he thought about it a while, and said, "I don't mind romance *per se*. But after making love for several hours at a clip, my mind does tend to wander on to other subjects."

"What other subjects?" I asked.

And he told me (and maybe you'd better write this down so you can offer to reveal the secret to your friends for their continuing elucidation, or possibly for money).

What this man told me was, "Basketball."

If you have been having "sexual problems" lately, you have probably been too embarrassed to talk about them, except to six or seven close friends at a public restaurant, or in a department store buying porch furniture.

You can't really put your finger on what the problem is, but you figure it has to have something to do with loss of romance or loss of spontaneity or loss of lust.

"Lust" is really the operative word here, but you're probably just too damn dainty to admit it. (In some Altaic languages the word for "lust" and the word for "romance" are exactly the same. How about *that*?) If a man thinks about many subjects, most of which are not *you*, while he is having sex with you, does that mean you are never going to get that old animal whatchamacallit back into your life together? Is this a national problem?

What the heck is lust, and why is it always so hard to call up when the situation seems to demand it?

Let's take the following worst-case example: There are times when a man's hormones become somehow "waylaid" en route to his pelvis. This is known in the English language as IMPOTENCE. (In the Altaic languages mentioned above, the word "impotence" is the same as the word for "death." This fact was revealed to Freud while on a train once, and Freud was reported to have said, "No kidding?")

The question has been raised: Is impotence worse for a man, or for the woman? If a man "performs" like a Lippizaner stallion 1,110 times, and fails the 1,111th time, the same words always flash into his mind: *That's It. I Must Be Gay.*

There is nothing you can say to make him feel better. There is nothing he can say to make *you* feel better. When he says, "This has nothing to do with you," you 1) don't believe him, or 2) wonder why on earth he invited you to be a witness at this debacle in the first place.

Unfortunately, men have all sorts of unrealistic role models surrounding them: guns, smokestacks, the Chicago Water Tower, the Chrysler Building, Twinkies, etc. These structures never lose interest in remaining rigid. A man feels that you would wish the same of him.

But *all kinds of things* can cause impotence in men: chemical depression, lack of job satisfaction, lack of hobbies, viruses, amnesia ("Where am I?" "Who is she?" "What is this?"), allergies, and unspecified alienation.

And sometimes, gosh darn it, men just plain DON'T FEEL LIKE IT. It just feels like too much *pressure.*

One phrase that gets bunted around a lot lately is PERFORMANCE ANXIETY. While women are sitting around being irrationally self-conscious about their bodies, men are lying around being irrationally self-conscious about what they are *doing* with their bodies. And are they doing it enough? And doing it *long* enough and *hard* enough and, you know, *lustfully* enough; and eventually their brains get tired of trying to sort it all out, and they just plain go to sleep.

How did a phrase like "performance anxiety" ever pick up any steam to begin with? It is perhaps appropriate for someone who is considering becoming an opening act for Itzhak Perlman at Avery Fisher Hall. Otherwise, it seems more than a little pretentious. After all, no matter how un-inspired a man may be during a particular romantic inter-lude, you are after all an audience of one, and you probably *won't walk out*—no, not even during the intermission or the slow movements. (He probably won't believe you, but it can't hurt to tell him this.)

I hesitate to tell you to try some kind of new-and-kicky technique to revive your man's flagging spirits. "New," "kicky" sexual techniques are becoming almost as tired a concept as adding curry to the tuna salad.

Being too good at sex, or trying too many novel ap-proaches can sometimes be a very *bad* idea. Your man will love every minute of whatever it is you are doing, but after-ward his eyes will follow you around the room. "Where did you pick that up?" he will say.

"Oh, something I've been meaning to try," you will say. Who are you kidding, Miss Nonchalant? Either you've been reading naughty books, or you did pick it up in exactly the sort of Somewhere he is referring to.

Sometimes the problem is you, and you alone.

Sometimes, you have a hard time separating "all the women you are" as they say in the feminine hygiene de-odorant ads.

Sometimes, when you are very preoccupied with life's more prosaic areas of endeavor, the idea of sex can seem downright *odd* to you.

Say that

- you've been in a steel-and-glass office complex all day working at a databank or word processor, in a subdued yet tasteful Halston suit and matching pumps. And when you come home from this environment,
- you are expected to lie stark naked on a mattress and sweat and make noises like a macaw in a Congolese rain forest.

You can't be blamed for occasionally asking yourself, "DO INTELLIGENT LIFE FORMS DO THIS?"

Do not feel guilty about having thoughts like these.

Part of the problem is that, in living with a man, sex becomes awfully Institutionalized. Just like men, you have an entirely rational voice in your brain that is saying, "Sex is much more enjoyable if you shouldn't be having it." And when you're living with someone you *"should"* be. "Shouldn't" you?

If you are a Catholic, life is especially difficult. Catholics do not like having sex before marriage, because they're not supposed to. They don't like having sex after marriage because they're *supposed* to. (Maybe when you were little, you met a lot of very confused Catholic boys. They would feel you up in the basement, then tell *you* to go to confession.) So no Catholic really knows what degree of sin he or she is living in, whether that sin should be enjoyed to the fullest, or only partially enjoyed.

No matter what your religion, if you are not having "sex problems" in your life right now, you are in the vast minority of Americans.

The more people have sex, the more they have sex problems. (The more you drive, the more you wear out your tire treads. We're talking simple mathematics. Simple probability.) It's not the end of the world.

But if you are living with a man, and he is sharing *your* (plural) sex problems with another person, and that person is not a qualified Sex Therapist but rather an aerobic dance instructor named Tina, then you require special attention here.

COPING WITH HIS INFIDELITY

LET'S say you've found out he's been fooling around.

You feel so bad, you can't see straight, you can't think straight, you can't walk straight; you've been spending a lot of time banging into things.

You should look on the bright side. You think *you* feel bad; imagine how *he's* feeling. All that guilt crammed into that craven human exterior. . . .

Somehow it is far, far worse for him than it would be for you. Women can handle guilt. They're on conversational terms with it; they take *lunches* with it: WOMEN have learned to live with guilt and, yes, to love it.

Men don't know the first thing about it until it socks them in the jaw.

And it usually creeps up on them from behind. One day they just plain drop the orange juice. They stick their pinky in a light socket. One night you're in bed together watching an anteater crawl up Johnny Carson's arm on *The Tonight Show,* and your man suddenly bursts into tears. And you know it's nothing *you* said.

It's guilt made manifest. And since you're not really involved in the logistics of his infidelity, your job is to put together what's left of him so he'll be usable at some point in the future. Usable to *you,* that is.

Remember, you're in a tricky situation. The more wise and understanding you are about his moral crimes, the more guilty he will feel. The more he will skulk about the house at baseboard level, the more he will chain-pop Rolaids, the more he will subconsciously attempt to maim himself with power tools.

It's not pretty, guilt. Of course he *deserves* to feel guilt.

But the challenge is to achieve a balance you can live with best. Here are some ways you can implement this:

- Let him off the hook. Do bad things. Have an affair with a guy who delivers hoagies for a living.
- Let the drama play itself out. Try to get him to spit out the whole sordid story. Say, "No matter how bad it is, I can handle it. Unless it's Mary-Beth. Please say it isn't Mary-Beth."
- Make him feel infinitely worse. Tell him you didn't really give him the best five years of your life. You were just kidding about that.

It will be very difficult for you to understand how a man that you felt close to could have lied, cheated, and gone behind your back, possibly for months and years at a time, all without your knowledge.

Even when he lost forty pounds, bought aviator glasses and a TV star-quality hairpiece, and stayed out every Wednesday night to learn "German for Opera Lovers," you never realized anything was amiss.

You will have to get over your amazement about How He Pulled It Off before you tackle the issue head-on.

Two things are for sure:

He will tell you that he doesn't deserve to be forgiven, but he hopes you forgive him.

He will tell you he doesn't deserve to be "taken back," but he hopes you'll take him back.

Then you will stare at him for a long minute and a half, just to watch him writhe.

And if he starts to cry, you'll be in serious trouble. Most of us hate to see a crying man, grown. He is very, very hard to resist.

Whatever you decide to do, you must look at a man's infidelity as a *learning experience*. Infidelity is usually a symptom of something; it is never an "accident"—whereas fidelity usually is.

Maybe if you had worn the black eye patch and the toreador pants when he asked you to, things would have been different. But there's no looking back now.

You must ready yourself to build a bright new future from the squalid ruins of your relationship.

CLOSENESS EXERCISES

MANY naive couples feel that their relationship actually has some kind of future *without* following the various "closeness exercises" one finds in today's popular magazines. But these couples are wrong. Relationships take work and practice. Like the piano, air conditioning, and dental hygiene, closeness needs *hands-on,* and occasionally knees-apart, experience. Here's a Beginning Closeness Exercise for the two of you to try.

1. Lie on the floor on your back, legs together, palms resting firmly on floor, knees to ceiling, mouth open, diaphragm flat.
2. Ask your man to do the same.
3. When he refuses to do the same, ask him why not.
4. When he tells you he would never agree to do a lot of queer, humiliating exercises out of some $1.95 magazine, and it'll be a cold day in hell before he'll ever lie down on the floor and make a damned ass of himself, burst into tears.
5. Tell him you want to go into Couple Therapy.
6. When he refuses to go into Couple Therapy, sob in short, rhythmic bursts; tell him you're really sorry you're acting the way you're acting, but you're probably getting your period, and you'll never act this way again.
7. When he tells you he sure as hell hopes you won't, tell him there's no reason to *swear* about it.
8. Go into bedroom and have sex.

(Repeat exercise three times.)

HOW ABOUT "COUPLE THERAPY"?

THIS is indeed a question for our age.

Therapy, in a world where religious leaders are Just a Bunch of Guys in Beanies, is an idea whose time has come.

It used to be that if you were having marital difficulties (read "humiliating sex problems"), you and your mate would go to visit a clergyman who was wise, avuncular, and a trusted member of the community. But sometimes sitting face to face with this awfully familiar person could be embarrassing. Could you really look him in the eye while wearing little white gloves and singing "A Mighty Fortress Is Our God," afterward?

That's why modern people in the know choose to go cry in front of a total stranger with a master's from NYU, who keeps looking at his watch.

Many people, who have never been in therapy, misunderstand what the process is all about. Therapy, of course, is not only for "crazy" people, but also for people whose brains need a little toning, firming, shaping, and tightening.

A therapist is not supposed to "care" about your problems. He is simply a technician—a user-friendly problem-solving *system*.

A therapist
- does not tell you what to do with your life: He lets *you* decide what you want to do with your life.

A therapist
- paraphrases the things you say, in a way that makes you realize how much more intelligent he is than you.

A therapist
- does not answer questions for you, but rather poses new

questions which *you* never would have been able to think up on your own.

He tells you that you are not thinking what you *think* you're thinking. A good therapist keeps his distance from you. The less he actually does, the more he wants you to pay him.

A "couple therapist" should be able to tell you if your relationship is "healthy." And what is a "healthy" relationship?

What do *you* think it is? Statistically, it is one where there is no undue dependence, little parental intrusion, complete mutual trust, and sex 4.5 times a week. (These four points are "ideals" of course. A couple in St. Petersburg, Florida, once achieved a perfect "four," but they died a week later.)

A therapist lays bare the "inner workings" of your relationship. Who wields the power? Who is the "Parent"? Who is the "Fascist"? Who is the "Big Cheese"? Who is the "Cottage Cheese"? Who is the "Little Tomato"? (You have to do all this before lunch.)

A therapist finds out about your *parents*. Especially when you say you don't want to talk about your parents. A therapist says, "*Why* don't you want to talk about your parents?" (And don't say anything *sarcastic*. It'll go on your final grade.)

A therapist will find out if you have chosen a man exactly like your father. (Which you never would have been able to figure out by yourself. You are *not intelligent enough*.) You will find out if you have chosen a man exactly like your mother. (You can't see it, personally. Your man cannot make grilled cheese sandwiches, and he does not squint when he talks.)

A therapist finds out who in your relationship has "unreasonable expectations." Who has "hidden agendas." Who is playing "Power Games." (There are a number of books on these subjects. Your therapist is very intelligent. He has read all of them.)

A therapist can serve as arbitrator in all the petty little disputes you and your man are inevitably embroiled in. He can help you decide

- whether toilet paper should unroll from down to up or up-to-down;
- whether pepper should ever go on French fries or onion rings;
- whether a need for a convertible guest sofa is a hidden cry for "unwanted relationship conflicts," also known as "guests."

THERAPY IS NOT PRETTY. You should be able to determine this from your therapist's choice of wall art. Many times you will be forced to uncover many *long-buried experiences*, which you buried for a very good reason. You will unbury your experiences, and your man will unbury his; and the experiences will sort of lurch about the room; and for a while your therapist's office will resemble the last scene from *Night of the Living Dead*. And just as things are getting good, he'll say, "We have to stop. But we have some *good material* here for next week. . . ."

I should warn you that, aside from being *unattractive*, therapy is also very *expensive*. You and your man will have to decide how you are going to pay for the sessions.

Should it be

- the one who's "craziest"?
- the one who's "richest"?
- the "eternal loser"?
- your parents? (Often a popular choice.)

Be sure to mention any "payment conflicts" to your therapist. Your therapist will not be embarrassed about discussing money; he will be very sensitive. The more sensitive he is about money, the more he'll want you to pay him.

Be sure to GIVE THERAPY A CHANCE TO WORK.

It takes time and effort and struggle and pain to really be ecstatic with your life.

"Is couple therapy worth it?" many troubled people have asked me.

The important thing is, what do *you* think?

ROLE MODELS

MANY of us, in times of personal need, turn to role models. They help us to know that someone is out there facing the problems, negotiating the same psychic terrain, baring their breasts to the same emotional slings and arrows. Etc., etc., etc.

Literature and popular culture are redolent with such role models. Our debts to them are incalculable.

The Ralph and Alice Kramden Guide to Living Together

If you watch "The Honeymooners" regularly, you will learn everything you ever need to know about living with a man. But don't watch Ralph Kramden—watch Alice. Alice Kramden is a genius.

The Honeymooners live in the ugliest room you'll ever see. It has a sink and a door; that's about it. Alice always wears a nice ponytail and a clean dress, and she's probably a pretty good cook and all, BUT SHE HAS A SMART MOUTH. She is married to a bus driver—a guy who only "gets off at the local stops," so to speak; the kind of guy who's not exactly upwardly mobile. And Alice's SMART MOUTH is the last thing he wants to hear at night.

This is what he says to Alice: "Do you want to go on a *trip*, Alice?" *"Do you want to go to the moon?"* Or simply, *"Bang! Zoom! To the Moon!"*

This unique combination of domestic violence and space travel is never a serious threat to Alice, because she knows Ralph will always embrace her at the end of the show and say, "Baby, you're the greatest." No one knows *how* she always knows this, but she does. That is why she is a genius.

She never has black-and-blue marks, or her arm in a sling, as most other WIVES WHO ARE ALWAYS RIGHT might have.

This is a very ambitious role model. If you are NOT A GENIUS, you may want to try something less risky.

There is only one Alice Kramden. She knows what she's doing.

The Henrik Ibsen Guide to Living Together

All women in Ibsen plays are failures at living with men.

They either walk out of the house in a huff, go insane, or blow their heads off with revolvers—while their menfolk stand around chewing on the horsehair furniture.

It is possible that these women's problems are hereditary —that being Norwegian, they are congenitally melancholy, or have goat cheese on the brain.

But many have said that Ibsen touches on universal truths in his work:

- Men are always the last to know what's going on around them.
- Men always say the worst possible thing, at the most IRONIC possible time.
- Ibsen women are always tormented by the question, "What is my *role* in life?" (Although they always know their lines.)

Fortunately, these problems are almost obsolete. We must bear in mind that in nineteenth-century Norway there were no self-help books for women. Norwegian women had no "support groups"—they just had melodramatic Grieg piano music and paintings of people screaming.

The Lucy and Ricky Ricardo Guide to Living Together

Like so many of Ibsen's heroines, Lucy Ricardo is a very frustrated woman.

Lucy wants to be in show business. But her husband, entertainer RICKY RICARDO, will not entertain the notion.

So Lucy resorts to lying, trickery, and illegal acts to achieve her ends. Along with her mostly unattractive cohort, ETHEL MERTZ, Lucy dresses like

- various female celebrities
- various vegetables, and
- various pieces of household furniture

in order to *fool* RICKY into allowing her her place in the sun.

These are acts of a desperate woman. A woman without shame, a woman clinging to her last shreds of self-respect.

And RICKY taunts Lucy, sometimes leading her along the garden path, making her *think* she is about to achieve her "big break."

Some nights he comes home and tells her CESAR ROMERO is coming to dinner. (Perhaps the arrival of minor Hispanic celebrities in *your* home is not cause for that much excitement, but try to imagine yourself in 1955.)

But Lucy's hopes are always dashed in the end.

She does give birth to a lovely child ("LITTLE RICKY") on the air in the course of her video tenure, and he seems to make Lucy happy, after a fashion.

But as in Ibsen's chilling drama *Ghosts*, the show's writers leave us with the nagging question:

"Will 'LITTLE RICKY' grow up to repeat the sins of his father?"

Will Lucy die a broken, embittered woman? Indeed, comedy has a dark side, and you should regard *I Love Lucy* as a cautionary tale.

The Fred and Wilma Flintstone Guide to Living Together

Even though the Flintstones live in the stone age, they are people who understand the GOOD LIFE, and live it to the fullest. Strangely, they have been ignored as role models for today's affluent young, and this is a serious omission.

- Wilma Flintstone wears great jewelry. When she wears rocks around her neck, they really are *rocks*. Wilma Flintstone was wearing seasonless suedes long before anyone ever heard of Diana Vreeland.
- The Flintstones live in a very ahead-of-its-time stone dwelling. (Merle Oberon had something like it in Mexico, shown in *Architectural Digest* once, but that was over a million years later.)

- Fred and Wilma never eat vegetables. Vegetables are too middlebrow a concept.
- Fred Flintstone was smart enough to get in on the ground floor of the petroleum industry—Flintstone was literally *creating* fossil fuels in his backyard, long before anyone had ever heard of Mobil or Exxon.

Fred and Wilma were living proof that in the absence of material wants, any relationship can flourish; as long as it's founded on the Bedrock of mutual trust.

The Starsky and Hutch Guide to Living Together

Starsky and Hutch are the greatest TV couple of all time.

One of them is blond and rugged and sort of cute and the other is brunette and cute and sort of rugged, and they are undyingly faithful to each other. Whenever one of them becomes interested in another (a woman, let's say), she always goes blind or catches a fatal disease, so that Our Boys never have to break up.

Starsky and Hutch are nice to black people and drive a Really Boss car and they never "dress up" for each other, because true love doesn't rely on artifice. And the way they flirt with each other, you know it's for keeps. Also, one of them always has a wacky hobby, such as biorhythm forecasting, so that the weight of police work won't encumber their buoyant, boyish spirits.

Starsky and Hutch represent an ideal you should strive for. It won't be easy. You have your work cut out for you.

The French New-Wave Cinema Guide to Living Together

Back in the fifties, when America was just discovering kinescopes, Cold War fever, and Speedy Alka-Seltzer®, the tireless French were flat on their backs *inventing* Living Together.

This is why French new-wave films of the fifties and sixties never look dated, even to today's carefree young. Pedal-pushers and harlequin sunglasses never die, after all. They just get remarketed.

Living Together à la française is easy, popular, and fun. You never have to learn any major lessons, or talk about anything important:

- Whenever it looks as though your relationship may reach a denouement, moodily light a cigarette and peer through the smoke.
- Then run away to Cap d'Antibes with a German.
- Then come back with a baby (not the German's).
- Then have a long argument against a white wall.
- Then steal a Citroen and have a long inner monologue about God and sex.
- Wear black eyeliner and striped pullovers.
- Let your man menace you. Menace him.
- Bring home a cat and pretend to let the cat menace both of you.
- Cut your hair like Jean Seberg's.
- End up marrying someone you don't love, because life is *la folie.*

The Mr. and Mrs. Macbeth Guide to Living Together

Macbeth was a Scottish king who ran into some witches in the woods one day, and they told him exactly what was going to happen in the next four acts of his life; and he believed them.

Trouble was, Macbeth was an ineffectual pantywaist from the word go, and didn't understand that he had to fulfill his *own* self-fulfilling prophecy. So his wife, Mrs. Macbeth, had to do this for him.

She was very irritated by having to take on his responsibilities such as polishing Macbeth's scabbard, bolstering Macbeth's ego, and stabbing Macbeth's dinner guests to death.

Predictably (the witches said this; not I), things ended badly for the Macbeths. Mrs. Macbeth had a severe stress reaction to the added responsibility in her life and killed herself with a sleeping potion. Macbeth was beheaded by some slaphappy Neighbor Kings, and the Macbeth Castle was put on the market.

Perhaps if Lady Macbeth had had some worthwhile *creative outlets* for her talents, things would not have gotten so far out of hand. I understand bargello was popular in twelfth-century Scotland, but Mrs. Macbeth never gave it a chance. Let this be a lesson to you.

The Samuel Beckett Guide to Living Together

Couples in Beckett plays always get on extremely well because, as they keep reminding each other, they have nowhere else to turn.

This life style is particularly advisable if

- you have large mounds of dirt that need to be moved, teaspoon by teaspoon, from one end of your living room to the other. Or,
- your aged relatives happen to be living in ashcans on the premises, and like to poke their heads up once in a while and say, "What's it all mean, eh?" and "What's to be done, eh?"

Try to keep your decor spare, and your conversations sparse.

Here's a good example of Beckett breakfast repartee:

"Milk?"

"Yes."

"Sugar?"

"Yes."

"There's a leak in the carport. The tropical fish aren't eating."

"A leak."

"Yes."

"The fish are dying."

"Yes."

"Dying."

"Yes. Floating."

"I don't know. What can we do?"

"I called the men from diPaolo's. They're not coming. I don't know."

You may think this life style is a tad on the dull side, and justifiably so. On the other hand, if your man and you are together because you really *do* feel a profound sense of Cosmic Displacement, and you are sharing a Silent Scream of Formless, Wrenching Angst, don't ever let anyone talk you out of it, you two crazy kids, you. . . .

4

Man
Made Perfect

DRESSING YOUR MAN, FROM THE INSIDE OUT

MEN like to walk around naked in the home, because it makes them feel like babies again, and few other experiences make them feel like babies again in a socially approved way. (Spitting up strained peaches at the office water cooler doesn't wash, for example.) You should not discourage casual home-grown nudity just because you're afraid of what Other People might think. Your man is continuing in a long, honorable tradition: Benjamin Franklin was an ardent nudist throughout much of his life. And Winston Churchill used to walk around naked late in his career. Having personally won World War II, issues like vanity, cellulite, and hair loss did not concern him.

Men like to be naked because they like to play with their Nether Parts. Not in any way that the Mormon church would take exception to, but just in a general, friendly-like sort of way. Here are some explanations assorted men have offered:

- "I like to make sure It's still there, you know?"
- "It's like a visit with a friend who's always home."
- "I once had a dream where It turned into a small cape pigeon and flew away to Rio, and it's terrified me ever since."

The world, in my opinion, would be a far better place if every man walked around the house as fully, holistically naked as the day he first sucked air. But on some truly dark day in male development, the concept of

Underwear

burst forth.

No one knows why women have always had the responsibility for wearing really attractive underwear. A man walking around the house in Fruit of the Loom briefs, even scrupulously white ones (which is seldom the case), is scarcely ever an alluring sight. Some men have even dallied with really aberrant forms, like sleeveless, V-neck, and mesh undershirts. No one knows who manufactures these strange and unsightly items. Certainly it is a plot, but its origins will probably never be traced.

Women fill their drawers with coquettish items like lace tap pants, push-up bras, and black garter belts, and in these garments they are likely to induce growls of approbation in even the most reticent male housemate. The best that can be said about a man in white cotton reinforced-crotch briefs is that he is probably *clean*. Semiclothed in this way, a man is but a halfway house on the road to complete selfhood. And yet he so often feels the need, yea, the inalienable *right*, to parade about the house with impunity in a depressing state of demidress. Or worse, in *socks*.

Most of us have memories of our fathers, possibly splayed out in front of a Chargers game on TV, in a pair of Hanes irregulars that our mother got him in a fit of proprietary affection at Sears the week before, and we thought to ourselves, "IF THIS IS SEX, WHAT WILL *TOTAL DISILLUSIONMENT* BE LIKE?"

I can offer you little reassurance in this area—when you choose to live with a man, you will unfortunately be forced to see the *man*, whereas others only see the *product*. There are no Standards and Practices that apply to the man himself; occasionally, you will have to view him through half-closed eyes.

Good luck.

Outerwear

The man who says he is uninterested in haberdashery is a dangerous commodity. There is many a man who feels that habitual, willful spiffiness is indicative of latent homosexuality and, thus, to be avoided at all costs.

What can you do?

It is true that you should never try to overdress a man, as if he were a Ken doll, a wedding usher, or other full-time stiff. Casualness means a lot to most men, and has throughout the ages. Why else are such cultural heroes as Lenin and Frank Sinatra always portrayed with raincoats over their shoulders?

If a man at least has taste (which is unfortunately a DNA-linked trait) you have something to *work* with, anyway. There are many dividends to living with a man who has good taste in clothes. Among them: If you are very good and well-behaved, HE MAY LET YOU WEAR THEM.

I'm not talking about anything kinky here. Most men's clothes nowadays are simply of higher quality than women's —built to last, and all that sort of thing.

Men's shirts, for example, are made in an exclusive suburb of Rome by naturally artistic *paesani e paesane*. Women's shirts are made in Korea by colorblind war orphans.

Wearing men's clothes, like any other substance addiction, should be entered into tastefully, and with discrimination. It is not *stealing*, after all, since you are trying to achieve an effect that is beneficial to you both. If you contrive to wear a man's oversized tuxedo shirt as a bathrobe, you may approximate the winsome, fetching look of a French *gamine*, and he may ravish you several times before breakfast. (Or, he may say, "Can the French *gamine* bit, Louise, and hand me my damn shirt." Don't get heavy-handed with men. They were not born yesterday, you know.)

We are talking, so far, on the *plus* side of men-and-clothes. Unfortunately, men who own and wear *inexcusable* garments are part of the gene pool, like all the rest of us— and it is just possible that you have settled on a guy who is a portrait of rectitude in most other areas, but whose choice of garments invariably reminds you of something you refused to let your father wear to Brownie Parents' Night in 1964.

A man can react in one of two ways to having no taste: 1) He can feel a deep, abiding, and highly appropriate sense of shame, which will last him all his days, and he will allow you to dress him. Or: 2) He will derive great pleasure out of sporting CERTIFIABLY LOATHSOME ensembles, knowing how strenuously you disapprove of them.

This latter behavior can be highly stressful for women who like to keep a high public profile. They often lash out in ineffective, even violent ways, and end up exacerbating the problem they are trying to solve. (Such as saying, "The way *you* look is a reflection on me, you know. And you don't even care." Of course he doesn't care. Any man who buys a tie with green hockey sticks on it in the first place, and expects to wear it in public, can hardly be expected to be sensitive to the feelings of others.)

Giving everything your man owns to Catholic Charities while he's at work is only sidestepping the problem. HE'S ALREADY A REPEAT OFFENDER. A TASTE FOR DOUBLE-KNITS, AN-TRON POLYESTERS, AND SMALL FLORAL PRINTS IS IN THE BLOOD.

You can, however, use positive reinforcement and idle threats to your advantage, *if you do it properly.* There is a right way and a wrong way.

Wrong: "*I* think you look really sexy in that subtle tweed jacket and those gray, uncuffed well-fitting trousers."

Right: "*Women* think you look really sexy in that outfit with the sexy tweed jacket and those sexy gray trousers."

Here are some general questions and answers regarding you and your man's wardrobe:

Q. Why did men ever start wearing plaid, and how can they be stopped before life loses its bearable qualities?

A. They probably cannot be stopped, but at least we can try to keep them away from young, impressionable children.

Q. Why do men wear sunglasses, sun visors, and rubber beach sandals indoors?

A. So that people will think 1) that they are from California, or 2) that they someday plan to go to California. Why they should want to create these impressions, no one knows.

Q. Do men know how hairy and frightening their toes look when they wear leather sandals, and how hairy and frightening their ankles look when they wear loafers without socks?

A. Yes, but they don't care.

Q. Is there any research being done on chemically inducing good taste in men, possibly while they are still in the fetal stage, in order to avert a lot of needless suffering by the women they will know in later life?

A. Laboratory rats, injected with certain substances, have been known to shy away from photographs of car salesmen and professional golfers, so there seems to be a lot of hope in this field, yes.

A LITTLE OFF THE TOP: THE INDIGNITY OF HAIR LOSS

MANY women foolishly believed that when Sean Connery stopped wearing his toupee, baldness would stop being an issue entirely. This, of course, did not happen.

Don't believe that thinning hair doesn't bother a man. You know that story about bald men being more virile? Do you know how hard bald men worked to spread that rumor? They worked *weekends* to spread that rumor.

Baldness is the first frontier of male vanity, and if you live with a man, it becomes part of your life, too.

Funny thing is, the whole problem doesn't bother him because of anything *you've* said. I can almost bet on it. You've probably been pretty sensitive about the issue. You've kept your mouth shut because you know men have no sense of humor about going even *sort of* bald.

Like as not, a man's *friends* have been making pithy little comments. They've made jokes in the locker room, or down at the club.

This is something you'll never fathom. You would never look a close friend in the eye and say, "You're looking quite the grizzled hag today, Betty."

But a man will tell another man *all* about his receding

hairline, and both will laugh uproariously, purporting to enjoy themselves, when in fact no enjoyment is taking place whatsoever.

There is a principle at work here you'll never understand: MEN TREASURE AND ZEALOUSLY GUARD THE RIGHT TO GET TOGETHER AND SAY TOTALLY INSENSITIVE THINGS TO EACH OTHER. It's part of being a man.

It is very likely that at some point in his life, your Balding Man will consider taking drastic action. He will start watching those late-night TV ads where guys wearing exciting-looking *hair substitutes* (they don't call them "toupees" anymore) do all kinds of sporty, active, virile things: swimming, skiing, horseback riding.

Do not attempt to understand these advertisements.

Your man was probably never interested in any of these activities before. Hair replacements contain remarkable chemicals that compel a man to go horseback riding.

Do not try to dissuade your man from investing in a hair substitute, if he really has his head set on it. (At best, he'll look like a has-been Las Vegas comedian in his new rug—you can even buy him a shiny new tuxedo or lime-green sports jacket to complete the effect.)

Better, really, to try a more modern realistic approach: Share with your man this list of famous personalities who have dealt with baldness in CREATIVE WAYS over the years. (And never say "BALDNESS," by the way. Say "hair attrition" or "gradual scalp emergence." Every little bit helps.)

Creative Bald Personalities

- Television producer NORMAN LEAR. Mr. Lear has a white sailor's hat that accompanies him on all personal appearances. He seems quite attached to it. Does Mr. Lear own or operate a sailboat? I address this question to the public at large.
- Sportscaster HOWARD COSELL. Mr. Cosell went to the time and expense of acquiring a hairpiece, when everyone *knows* that on a bright day he could reflect signals to Venus off the top of his head. He is saying, "I know what *you* know; but perhaps younger generations will come to think I *really* look this way."

- Actor PERNELL ROBERTS. Except while guest-starring on old episodes of "Mission Impossible," you'll never catch *this* guy in a hair replacement. He even does wine commercials, wearing a V-neck sweater, with his chest hair showing. He is saying, "Hair on my *head* would be an embarrassment of riches."
- Former French monarch MARIE ANTOINETTE, former Scottish monarch MARY STUART, former British tart-turned-monarch ANNE BOLEYN. All these ladies had their heads shaved immediately preceding their executions, so that their royal tresses would not get in the executioner's way.

As you can see, baldness is much more serious in the case of women.

A Note on Male Body Image in General

All kinds of things are happening in the area of BODY IMAGE EQUALITY. Surveys show that in 1984, men are as likely to bore you about how fat they are as women are. Now you get to say, "Yeah, but in clothes it hardly shows at *all*," to men you barely know at cocktail parties.

It's not that men are truly *vain*, mind you. It's not as though they want to be *pretty*. They wouldn't mind looking like Johnny Cash, say. Johnny Cash has a lived-in face—it even has a *hole* in it. He's never had the hole filled. Johnny Cash could have his dentistry done from the outside.

Guys like that devil-may-care approach to vanity. Guys don't want to look like Tab Hunter or Richard Simmons or Prince Valiant. However, you should know that EVERY MAN, AT LEAST ONCE IN HIS LIFE, HAS LIED ABOUT HIS HEIGHT.

This shouldn't really bother you unless you are some kind of weird stickler for statistical accuracy in your men. If you are very good at trigonometry, you can measure your man's shadow as he stands on a patio at high noon, then run to your room; figure out the cosine of his loafers; and do some quick triangulation.

Somehow, this seems like coarse behavior to me. So what if he lies, and it's obvious. If your mother, in flats, towers over him, and he still claims to be five feet eleven, this is known as a victimless crime; and it's very tacky of you to call him on it.

THE CARE AND FEEDING OF THE INFIRM MAN

YOU don't necessarily have to marry a man anymore to get him in sickness and in health. Even if you're Just Spending a Lot of Time Together, there's a good chance that the next time the man in your life drops in his tracks—from the flu, food poisoning, softening of the arteries—you'll be elected to play Florence Nightingale. You can pick one of many reasons for this: 1) Adversity brings people closer together; 2) men are more willing these days to admit to physical weakness; 3) if you don't do it, someone else will. (Men are often extremely alluring when they can't move their extremities.)

Now this is the thing about human malady: Biologists will tell you that, statistically, men get sicker than women. But women figured this out by themselves a long time ago. Men are much better piners-away than women are. They have a far more impressive arsenal of creative moans. And why is this true? Simple. Women's bodies are always doing excruciating, uncalled-for things, at least every twenty-eight days, and often more frequently. Nonspecific twinges and *douleurs* are Our Lot. And since, for example at a job interview, it's almost never good policy to say, "Excuse me, mind if I double up in agony on your couch?" women have learned to do the next least destructive thing—stifle.

Men have no such talent. They learned to have no such talent early in life for this very good reason: It would have deprived their mothers of one of the great, shining moments of motherhood. The chance to say, "Get into your jammies. I'll take care of everything." No matter what he says he wants in life, no man will ever tire of the words, "Get into your jammies. I'll take care of everything."

How do you know when your man is halfway to the here-after and in need of ministration? Here are some powerful warning signs:

1. You get up in the morning and he is blocking the door to the bathroom with his prostrate body. You ask if there is anything you can do. He says no.

2. You are sitting at breakfast and you ask him if he wants the Spanish omelette you didn't finish. He stares ethereally off into space and says "*I* don't care. . . ."

3. His skin begins to take on the color of Roquefort cheese. His gestures become feeble, his eyes bereft of all hope. He checks his glands at regular intervals.

If he does any of these things, there's a very good chance that he's sick. He may not tell you. He *probably* won't tell you. This is why: SICK MEN ARE GREAT BELIEVERS IN FORM. They don't want to tell you precisely what contagion is sucking at their vitals. They want you to *guess*. This usually takes the form of multiple choice (and it can take hours. Grab a sandwich first). A sample:

Q. Where is it? In your head?

A. Yeah. I don't know. Yeah.

Q. And your stomach.

A. I guess. Yeah.

Q. How about your throat?

A. My throat. Yeah, my throat.

As you can see, sick men are more than willing to meet you halfway in the initial diagnosis. In fact, that's the easy part. But let's say that he's already called the office and ascertained that his presence won't be required. His duties discharged, he is now free to collapse somewhere and HE WILL—probably facedown on the rug so as to minimize the possibility of breathing.

It is your job to get him somewhere he won't be found later in an advanced state of rigor mortis by the ambulance corps, who'll blame you. You've got to get him under the covers.

And once you've gotten him tucked in, he will want you to do some, or all, of these things:

1. Turn on the TV. He will then want to know why he's

seen this particular episode of "The Munsters" nine times. You'd better have an answer.

2. Make him soup/cream of wheat/cinnamon toast with the crust cut off.

3. Call the doctor. Now this is important: The less ambulatory he is, the more he will insist he can get to the doctor's by himself. No one knows why this is. It's just a law. You say to him, "But, Mitchell, no one can walk or drive a car while lapsing in and out of consciousness. Let's rethink this." You have not understood this law: MALE BEHAVIOR DURING ILLNESS IS DICTATED BY YEARS OF WATCHING VICTOR MATURE MOVIES. It is important for him to be agonized-yet-tough. So you've got to compromise here. You take him to the doctor, but later let him crawl on his stomach to the refrigerator for a turkey leg. He'll know that your heart is melting at the sight of the veins standing out on his forehead—that's what love is all about.

Rules to Keep on Hand

There are certain rules in dealing with the Infirm Man that require plain common sense. For example, if he asks you "How do I look?" under no circumstances should you tell him the truth. Other rules take practice to master. If he always liked raisin toast complete with raisins, now he will want the raisins removed. If he was always groomed to the point of obsession, now he will allow plentiful and dangerous amounts of facial stubble to surface, especially in places you didn't know he had follicles. If he always slept in the nude, you will suddenly find him in possession of the most hideous bile-colored pajamas you have ever seen, and he will want to wear them.

Now here's the true test of devotion: How do you know when you need to stay home from work to take care of him? He will never *ask* you to. As you are going out the door, he will make a noise that sounds like the death rattle of a wildebeest, but he will never *ask* you to stay. What you have to decide is, whatever It is, do you want to get It?

If It's going around anyway, why fight It? In fact, germs-

at-large could work in your favor. . . . YOU COULD GET IT
FIRST. Picture it: At your desk at eleven o'clock one morning
you realize you're not yourself. By three o'clock, every mol-
ecule in your body is screaming "Pack it in! Pack it in!" You
decide to go home. You make it to the bus. You board the
bus. You actually make it to your door. And there—because
this is real life, and this isn't your lucky week—is your com-
panion in life, *already* home, *already* checking his vital signs
with the air of a practiced diagnostician. You will assess the
situation. But not for long, because you *know* what you will
do. You will say, "Get into your jammies. I'll take care of
everything." Okay, you'll do it because, by gosh, you *love*
this guy. But also because you know God is looking down
and keeping a scorecard on who the stronger sex really is.

Dentistry and Your Man: The Cruel Truth

WOMEN sometimes sort of like the dentist, if the truth be
told. Here's a guy with immaculately clean hands, standing
with his pelvis pressed against your beating heart. He is
talking to you in a soothing voice, gently wiping your
cheeks, looking into your eyes, saying things like, "Great,
you're doing just great. . . ." and he gives you drugs whenever you want them.

Admit it. This is ten times more pleasant than most of the
dates you've had in recent years.

Most men are perfectly willing to make dentists' appointments, as long as they don't have to *keep* them. Keeping
dentists' appointments, most men feel, is an unnecessary
test of true manhood. Sure, any little *kid* can sit through a
root canal, knowing he's going to get a three-way decoder

ring or a rubber dinosaur or even a "Good boy, Biffy" from the dentist's lovely nurse.

But your grown guy says to himself, "What's in it for me, eh? A lifetime of dazzling smiles? The grudging respect of my peers? Forty percent fewer checkups? *Pat Boone* probably has that. *Include me out.*"

Also, he wonders about the moral justification of having another grown male fingering his gums. Dentistry, as we have seen, is a highly intimate, personal act. It's every bit as personal as being bathed by geishas on Honshu, except that your guy's dentist is probably a guy named Mel with thick thumbs and carpeting on his walls.

And then there's the matter of pain. Not only do men object to Novocain; they object to being asked if they *want* Novocain. It's like being asked if they want a blindfold before facing a firing squad. They figure that other guys can Take It, and so can they.

It is not known whether any man has actually died from dentistry, or more particularly from the stress of pretending he doesn't *fear* dentistry. There have been cases of insanity, hair turning white overnight—that sort of thing. Nothing you haven't heard about over a campfire late at night at scout camp. It's no laughing matter. There is no clear reason why the same guy who can sit through *Return of the Flesh Wogs* three times on his VCR refuses to accede to an afternoon's worth of necessary dental hygiene.

But one thing's for sure: If you don't think about his teeth occasionally, he won't think about his teeth *ever,* except to bite them into doughnuts and flash them at flight attendants. Living with a man's mouth is as taxing as living with the rest of his body put together. But if you do it right, just look at it as one more thing his mother can thank you for.

GETTING THROUGH TO MEN: THE INCREDIBLE SULK

MEN are often bewildered when, quite early in a relationship, you mention casually that they've been ignoring you for the last three weeks, and is it anything you've said, or are they just going through a phase?

Many men go running to their therapists or best friends, like irate consumers: "When she said she wanted *me*," they point out, "she didn't say anything about *talking, too*."

When you've been through this enough, you come to realize a cornerstone principle in living with a man:

Talking is extra. Like snow tires. Like rear-window defoggers. IT IS NOT INCLUDED IN THE LIST PRICE OF A MAN.

This puts you in a particularly difficult position.

If a man never tells you what he is thinking, *how are you ever going to know?* Should you guess? Should you offer him a series of true-and-false options? Should you read his tea leaves? Should you strike him, hoping to draw blood? (This is frustrating, after all. It is a *hard subject.*)

All the great courtesans of Europe were trained never to ask a man, "What are you thinking?" And they were rewarded many times over for their forbearance. With bracelets, even.

But sometimes you cannot help worrying about this poor blighter, who is pointedly mooning around the perimeters of your life. Sometimes you try to *narrow down* the problem. *For sure*, he's:

- fantasizing about some Bad Scandinavian women;
- hungry;
- bored;
- troubled about alimony payments;
- trying to remember the words to "Begin the Beguine";

- convinced he's gay;
- worried about the Sea Hawks possibly trading Zorn;
- plagued by hemorrhoidal itching and swelling;
- asleep.

Narrowing down the problem will probably help *you* sleep better. His end of it is just beginning, alas.

But you have to give a man "the space inside his head." Remember Blondie and Dagwood from the comics? Blondie couldn't stand to see Dagwood sprawled on the couch, lost in reverie or slumber or sordid sex fantasies. It wasn't just that she needed the storm windows installed. She wanted the piece of his soul that she was losing. (This is pretty cerebral stuff, I know. If you want to know a *lot* more about it, you should subscribe to *Psychology Today*. Or *Mademoiselle*.)

You can't hate a man when he crosses the moat and pulls up the drawbridge. If you try to scale his sides (note how well a MEDIEVAL METAPHOR works here), he'll pour offal on you and utter curses. And it's not just that—men honestly believe that women are very *smart*. They really do. They think that you already know the essential things about them.

Why Men Never Want to Have "A Serious Talk"

For some guys, the words "we have to have a serious talk" are grounds for gunning up the Harley and driving all night to Utah without stopping for breakfast.

Why is Serious Stuff so scary to men? Some say seriousness reminds them of church, or the time in sixth grade when the teacher yelled at the whole class for picking on blind people. Men carry these experiences around with them, and they fester.

Men are not comfortable with cold realities and naked truths. Men prefer to have their truths varnished. (This is why they were forced to take wood shop in the eighth grade. They learned to sand, plane, and lacquer truths; while girls learned to hem napkins and create fruit D-Zerta molds.)

Most men have been trained Never to Want to Talk

STEPHANIE BRUSH

About Anything Serious from a very early age: They realized at some point in their young lives that they would have to stop running to Mom every time they picked a scab wrong or fell down. They felt betrayed by life, and abandoned, when this happened. They felt they could never trust a woman again.

So you become the Nazi for a Day when you try to Get Serious with them. They see you in their mind's eye wearing little jackboots and a gun belt and a monocle; pistol-whipping them into submission. (*"Talk,* you dog! Is our relationship going down the tubes? Should we see Brenda and Raoul on Wednesday night? Do you like my suede shoes better, or the gray pumps? Am I getting huge around the hips? *Talk."*)

Sometimes men will play along with Serious Stuff. "Yeah, you're right," they say. "I'm glad you brought that up," they say. And you part friends, and realize some time later that you didn't reach any conclusions at all. These talks are to your emotional state what Chinese food is to your digestive tract. An hour later, you're saying, "Wait a minute; did I swallow anything, or didn't I?"

The worst thing you can possibly do, when it comes to a Serious Topic, is to bring it up just before going to bed. THE MINUTE YOU SAY TO A MAN, "I THINK WE'D BETTER CLEAR THIS UP BEFORE WE GO TO SLEEP," HE IMMEDIATELY GOES TO SLEEP. But women have been doing this for eons, and they're probably never going to stop.

Phone Therapy

In light of Man's continuingly spectacular lapses in interpersonal communication, women have begun to realize that they have some recourse.

You may be one of those souls who has established a regular, therapeutic talk extravaganza with a close female friend on the telephone. You do it because you need a friend, and your friend's voice soothes you almost as much as the sound of *your* voice—but mostly, you do it to drive Him crazy. You always talk to this friend when your man is in the room, listening.

You will need, for example, to tell your friend what you wore to the wingding you attended the night before.

- You will need to tell her what color it was.
- You will need to tell her whether you had shoes to match.
- You will need to tell her whether the heels were low or high.
- You will need to specify the height of the heels, in inches.
- You will then describe the shoes you did *not* wear, as an interesting compare-and-contrast exercise.
- You will need to describe your hair on the night in question.
- You will need to specify your weight on the night in question.

This is the point where most men sigh and throw up their hands in an extremely dramatic way and make hand signals and point to watches. They pretend to be holding small semaphore flags. They pretend to choke, and perform the Heimlich maneuver on themselves.

IF YOU ARE VERY FOOLISH, YOU WILL GET OFF THE PHONE AT THIS POINT. He will then retire to the bedroom where there is a hockey game in progress and ignore you for the next two hours.

Cash Machine Therapy

One often-overlooked source of comfort you might consider is the common corner cash machine. A lot of desperate, untalked-to women have close, intimate relationships with their automatic tellers (AMTs) these days.

Cash machines always have something nice and personal to say.

"HELLO," they always say. "HOW MAY I HELP YOU?"

And when you tell them, they are always so patient.

"JUST A MINUTE," they say. "I'M WORKING ON IT."

They don't *have* to tell you they're "working on it." They simply want you to know they haven't deserted you; they haven't gone to sleep or into a programmed sulk or something.

A cash machine never says, "I SAID I'M 'WORKING ON IT,' DAMMIT."

A cash machine never says, "GET OFF MY BACK WHILE I'M 'WORKING ON IT,' OKAY?"

A cash machine never says, "YOU KNOW, YOU SOUND MORE LIKE YOUR MOTHER ALL THE TIME."

The minute a cash machine learns to say, "I'VE ENJOYED GIVING YOU THIS MONEY. YOU SEEM LIKE A VERY NICE PERSON. DO YOU HAVE ANY PLANS FOR TONIGHT?" men are going to be in very big trouble.

THE STRESSED MAN

"LIFE got tougher," says the Excedrin ad. "We got stronger."

It's true. Actually, you should know that a consortium including Bristol-Myers, Johnson & Johnson, Procter & Gamble got together in the late 1950s and conspired to *make* life tougher so they could sell more painkillers. And so far, it's worked.

In the future we can expect to see caffeine-free painkillers, sodium-free painkillers, and diet painkillers. (For when you can't zip your Calvins, and immediately get a headache.) Also, lemon-y painkillers, and INTERNATIONALLY FLAVORED painkillers. (Actress CAROL LAWRENCE favors cappuccino-flavored painkillers.)

There are many factors in life that cause stress. They are called "stressors." (Just as you put your clothes in a "dressor" and the person who does your pants is called a "pressor.")

People live together so that they can reduce each other's stress levels. "I need to come home and have someone's shoulder to cry on," say many women. With today's seasonless, easy-care fabrics, crying on shoulders can be accomplished with a minimum of maintenance. And now that men are permitted to cry too, whole new vistas of bathos in the home are opening up.

We react to stress by breaking out in hives. Some of us have miniature psychotic breaks and imagine we are Empress Maria Theresa of Austria. Men run more toward renting a Ford Country Squire and going out to gun down Campfire Girls and dogs. Stress-related crimes of this magnitude have never been within the scope of women. Women ask dumb questions like, "If I had a semiautomatic weapon and several rounds of ammo, would they fit in the closet, between my shoe trees, for future use?"

Male anger is comparable to a passel of fissionable atoms. You are never really sure when something's going to start a chain reaction in him—when he'll stop being Your Guy and start being a Public Nuisance. (Should you suggest that the neighbors stage evacuation drills? Will he "internalize" his stress, merely throwing his burritos out the kitchen window; or will he hot-wire the fish tank to watch the guppies' eyes pop out?)

Having violent confrontations in bars is one socially approved way men have of handling stress. A man argues for a half-hour or so, usually with a close friend; many epithets are uttered, then one or both men return home to fetch a firearm of some kind, in order to settle the matter in the Manly Way recorded on police blotters across the nation.

(Women worry too much about protocol ever to pull off one of these moves successfully. A woman says, "How do I know the object of my wrath is going to sit around and *wait* for the fireworks to start?" And she feels like a damn clod saying, "Excuse me, Betsy—stay right here on this bar stool while I go home and get my illegal handgun."

Cardiologists are now able to actually pinpoint which men have ONE-OF-THESE-DAYS-YOU'D-BETTER-GET-OUT-OF-MY-WAY personalities. It behooves you to see whether your man fits into any of these eight categories, and to CHILL HIM OUT, to the best of your ability, if he does.

STEPHANIE BRUSH

The Eight Signs of High-Stress, or Type-A, Behavior

1. *Moving, eating, or walking rapidly.* When you are on your way to the movies, does he try to rush you by walking a block ahead of you? Does he try to rush you by arriving for the nine o'clock show at seven o'clock? A.M.? Does he virtually inhale baked chickens? Does he pace the floor and work up a sweat while watching television? While sleeping?
2. *Hurrying the ends of sentences.* Does he finish sentences for you but forget to finish his own? Does he finish other people's sentences, including those of people on television? Does he finish sentences in books?
3. *Feeling guilty about relaxation.* Are you tired of hearing excuses like, "When this Nicaragua Thing is settled, maybe we'll take a vacation"? Is he convinced he hears his office phone ringing when you're at a flea market in Tunis?
4. *Trying to increase work over ever-shorter time periods.* Is he fond of saying things like, "Rome wasn't built in a day, but then they didn't have a manager like *me* around to kick their butts, did they?"
5. *Acquiring objects rather than enjoying them.* Does he insist he needs a Dynamic Range Expander for his stereo, when you live in a one-room apartment, in a hospital zone? Does he bring home a chlorinator and a diving board on sale, when you don't have a pool?
6. *Relating success to time, that is, the speed-is-everything syndrome.* Does he want to do everything according to his quartz chronometer, an egg timer, or a stopwatch? Everything?
7. *Impatience.* Does he never settle on *one* radio station? Does he fetch bones for the dog because the dog has an attitude problem?
8. *Not listening to the opinions of others.* Do the Opinions of Others cause little beads of sweat to pop on his brow? Does he rend his garments and say, "Who cares what Leo thinks?" When you know that indifference to the opinions of Leo is folly?

If you have answered "By God, yes," to at least three of these questions, then you are living with a banners-flying Type-A man.

You can't really control him morally or legally; but you can put some lead in his socks *chemically*. It is the ultimate irony of the Type-A man that he wakes up in the morning needing to be scraped off the ceiling, *then* says, "Hey, where's my coffee? It's *late!* Where's my coffee?"

Give some serious thought to

Decaffeinating Your Type-A Man.

There's been a lot of discussion about this subject on the TV airwaves lately.

Women in commercials are always tricking their man into forcible decaffeination. (He has already become suspicious since the day she Changed His Sausage; a prevailing trend in the late seventies.) Women in commercials trick their men into many things. Men in commercials are Bad Rabbits and never seem to know what's good for them.

First, you must figure out what you're up against:

- He's had too much caffeine if he wants to sing camp songs at the breakfast table.
- He's had far too much caffeine if he calls up United Airlines at 6 A.M., just so he can argue with the recording.
- He's had dangerous amounts of caffeine if your mother calls and he talks to her, asks her how she is, and tells her he's been thinking about her.

Life would be wonderful if an elderly, respected TELEVISION ACTOR would walk into your home at any of these points, chuckle ruefully, and say, "Why so *nervous,* Richard?" And this actor would recommend a calming morning beverage for your man, then pack up his sound crew and toddle off into the sunrise, leaving the two of you to live destressedly ever after.

But this only happens to *other people,* chosen at random from the nation's Census Department computer banks.

MIDLIFE CRISIS

MAURICE Chevalier used to sing a song called "I'm Glad I'm Not Young Anymore."

Maurice Chevalier's straw boater was probably pressing on his brain at the time.

No man is glad he's not young anymore. And the moment it begins to filter through to his brain that Not Young will probably be a permanent state in his life, a man starts to reflect on all the things he's probably missed out on. These reflections may involve a racing ketch, a best-selling novel, or a set of nineteen-year-old Hawaiian triplets—the experience seems to be unique to each man. But the name of this phenomenon is always the same: Midlife Crisis.

Today's man is very highly evolved—far more so than his early twentieth-century counterpart. He no longer waits until his children leave home before he enters his first midlife crisis. He no longer waits to have children. Nowadays the onset of midlife crisis can occur moments after the onset of puberty. Men in their teens and twenties nowadays reach a serious midlife crisis when they decide to quit their jobs as box boys and legal assistants and become Jedi Masters.

It is traditionally Man's place in the universe to ask the question, "WHY AM I HERE?" (It has traditionally been Woman's place to ask the question, "Why am I fat?" Women have traditionally been too busy sucking in their cheeks, trying to resemble LAUREN HUTTON, to bother with the riddle of existence.)

A man begins to dream of lost adventures, Lost Horizons, at a certain age. He thinks of deep-sea diving and the high tor—he feels he *should* be hanging from a crampon somewhere on Annapurna or Dhaulagiri. (Women think a crampon is something negatively related to the menstrual cycle, which is why they rarely distinguish themselves in feats of mountaineering.)

You can always tell that a man is reaching his Crisis when he buys reflector sunglasses, just so he can commute to his job outside La Jolla: when he buys a Barcalounger and a subscription to *National Geographic,* and not just so he can look at the breasts of virgins from Zimbabwe. He wants to span the globe—to Make Tracks. He wants to become an oceanographer (because he thinks they have the most even suntans of anybody) and he wants to grow a huge sandy beard and read biographies of Gauguin. He sneaks copies of *Moby Dick* into the bathroom.

But midlife crisis does not have to disrupt both your lives indefinitely. The vast majority of mild-mannered, "maturing" men simply resign themselves to a life of thwarted hopes and silent, bootless internal cries. Sometimes they thoughtfully lay down the evening paper and pad on over to the local supermarket to haunt the frozen dinners section. There are Bad Women here, wearing form-fitting blouses, and their erectile tissue is behaving in shameful and thought-provoking ways.

A man looks at this and says, "Hmmm."

And then he buys turkey 'n' stuffing entrée and trots resignedly home.

GETTING YOUR MAN TOGETHER AND TAKING HIM ON THE ROAD

You can add color to your man's humdrum existence (and, heck, to yours in the bargain) by occasionally taking him on the road for some sort of joint holiday. But first, beware that vacation preferences are tricky shoals to navigate.

The year you tell him that a "Loire Valley XVIIth Century Tapestries Tour" might be sort of a kick, he looks at you blisteringly and walks out of the room.

And the year he enthusiastically talks up the Royal Canadian Ice Hockey Hall of Fame in Flin Flon, Manitoba, you voice a preference for being strangled and thrown in a ditch; and you both sit and glare at each other, saying, "Okay, let's just forget the whole thing. Let's just sit home and watch *television* all month."

Most couples end up alternating years. Here are some of the more exciting possibilities in LIVING-TOGETHER TRAVEL.

Motor Trips

More and more women these days are proud of their driving.

We have role models like Janet Guthrie and Cha Cha Muldowney; we can read an odometer with the best of them, and, yes, EVEN CHANGE A TIRE ON A DARK AND STORMY NIGHT.

None of this means he's ever going to let you drive when you really, really want to; I just wanted to pass these advances along to you.

There are two things you should always bear in mind when it comes to Men on the Road. The first is that every man has said, at least once in his life, the following words: "WHAT ARE YOU WORRYING ABOUT? I'M A GREAT DRIVER."

He will say this irrespective of the speed he is traveling, or your *concern* about the speed he is traveling. He will say this after having just cut off three Hell's Angels, who are now making motions in the rearview mirror which involve the application of lug wrenches to your windpipes. He will say this as he is driving backward along an expressway, trying to get back to an exit he passed four miles ago. At eighty mph.

(Einstein was a great driver, or so he used to tell people. He used to test his theory of relativity by driving so fast his passengers would start to age backward. It gave them something to talk about, back in Zurich.)

The second thing you should remember is that MEN DO NOT BELIEVE IN ASKING FOR DIRECTIONS WHEN THEY ARE LOST. They just turn up the Chet Atkins on the car radio, roll up the windows, and keep on driving.

This includes if you are driving through a neighborhood where the people look as if they learned armed robbery while still in their strollers, and are now strictly into murder and cannibalism. This includes if the last ladies' room you visited had a torso and a forearm in the waste basket.

"It doesn't matter where we *are*—that's not the concept," he explains patiently. "I am focusing on where we are *going*."

This is known as Zen navigation.

Activity Vacations

Some couples choose to plan their vacations around specific *activities,* on the assumption that shared interests will bring them closer together.

Take ski weekends and tennis camps, for example. Few men feel lukewarm about these two activities. If a man is very good at tennis and skiing, he loves tennis and skiing.

Unfortunately, no two people ski or play tennis at exactly the same level. And many men try to rectify this discrepancy by finger-pointing, blame-passing, and exaggerating. If a man happens to be very *bad* at tennis and skiing, he will find a way to convince you that it is *your fault.* And he will suffer many subtle private agonies.

- Men, for example, do not like to acknowledge the existence of courses labeled "beginner." They prefer names like "preintermediate" and "subexpert." For this reason they often shun Formal Instruction, when Formal Instruction is clearly indicated.
- Most men object to ski and tennis instructors on principle. Ski and tennis instructors have an insufferable brand of ready charm, expensive dental work (although they always claim they were born that way), and unacceptably well-muscled inner thighs. Men are very suspicious of this sort of thing.

If *you* are very bad at tennis and skiing, at least there is some future to your relationship. With work, men feel, you can be made useful; and men are always sure that your lack of enthusiasm is for all the wrong reasons.

Let's say you hate skiing because you're afraid of chairlifts. Once the two of you are safely aloft, your man will attempt to allay your fears by jumping up and down, pretending to fall off the chair, making death jokes, and trying to nibble your ears. If you tell your man you are cold, he will tell you that *he* is not cold, and *it* is not cold, and that therefore you are mistaken. Men think cold is manly. Men with blue lips always think they look like Admiral Peary or Roald Amundsen, whereas women with blue lips are always sure they look like corpses. (Mostly because they do.)

If you are very unskilled at a sporting activity, you can unselfishly agree to let your man go off on his own (a bit difficult in the case of doubles tennis, but many men try to pull this off) and you can meet him for a snifter of something at the end of the day. And then of course you can have sex.

(Many people overlook sex in *itself* as a vacation activity because it doesn't cost anything and it requires no equipment, lessons, or driving time to speak of.

Some have compared the thrill of sex to solo flying, or high-speed auto racing. But sex does not require sunglasses or protective headgear, and if you fail at it, you don't get carried off on a stretcher by a lot of smug guys in asbestos jumpsuits.

Just something to think about.)

Boat Trips

You should always be on your guard if a man wants to buy, or rent, a sailboat.

Men love sailing. Women endure sailing.

Men tend to look quite attractive while they're sailing. They look sort of spunky and collegiate in Topsiders.

Women look *short* in Topsiders.

Once a man boards a sailboat, many things about his True Nature surface immediately:

- He will demonstrate his innate ability to Take Control.
- He will grommet himself permanently to the captain's seat with a foreign beer in his hand, the afternoon light gently burnishing his golden curls.
- Anything that involves lurching around the deck in high winds like a spastic, he will ask *you* to do. He will ask you not to throw up while there are other yachtsmen in view, and if you are not a Blonde with Legs, he will wish very much you were a Blonde with Legs; but he'll try not to make you feel inadequate about it.
- He will call you "babe" and "doll" and other sporting appellations as he tacks and beams; and you will stretch your lips over your teeth in an attitude reminiscent of a smile, and share the wondrousness of the experience with him. To the best of your ability.

Note on Ocean Cruises

Before you consider taking a fabulous OCEAN CRUISE, remember this: There is a very popular American television show that takes place aboard a cruise ship. You know the one I'm talking about. And maybe this program subliminally influenced you in a decision to rekindle your romance on the high seas.

But bear this in mind—the two people you *think* you see pledging their undying love in front of moonlit waves in the Pacific are actually standing in front of a rear-screen projection unit somewhere in Burbank. *They never even met each other before this episode was filmed.* Unless of course they were on the same show last year, in a different plot line about a

beekeeper who falls in love with a wacky female parole officer played by CHARO.
DOES THAT SHATTER YOUR ILLUSIONS?
Or, try this: YOU WILL GET FAT ON A CRUISE, EVEN THOUGH YOU SAY YOU WON'T. (So will he, but it won't bother him as much.)

Destination: Europe

PARIS

Paris was built by men, but not *for* men. Gene Kelly is the only American man who deserves to have his name associated with Paris. (We will not even *discuss* Hemingway here. You cannot tell me that in all those evenings at *Le Select* he was not actually fantasizing about boning a trout in Idaho. The only thing that Hemingway ever enjoyed in Paris was going to the men's room with Scott Fitzgerald and comparing Sizes.)

For most men, the only redeeming feature of Paris is the women. Men window-shop in Paris. French women like to wear overt symbols of American culture: *les jeans, les extrême-ment-tight jeans,* etc. French women do not steal men. They *eat* them. They have very pointy teeth, which is why they never smile (at least not at *you,* anyway).

There seems to be some kind of mythological significance to the term "French whore." Are "French whores" better at what they do because they're whores, or because they're French? The term probably has about as much cultural significance as "French cleaning" and "French cuffs." But try to tell a man that. You cannot explain to him that the French are hopelessly behind the times sexually. When was the last time the French produced a really good piece of pornography?

All the great minds of France, who should be supporting professional pornographers, are at work in the *Académie Française* trying to keep words like *le cruise control* from creeping into the language.

MEN: AN OWNER'S MANUAL
ROME

People from all over the world travel to Rome on religious pilgrimages, but all too many of them waste their time in places like the Vatican. Nowadays, the worship of FINE LEATHER FOOTWEAR has replaced Catholicism in most with-it Italophile homes. You must explain to your man that:

- your worship must take place in mornings *and* afternoons, along the via Condotti and the via del Corso, with perhaps a short break for *panini* or something;
- you cannot ever be expected to wear American shoes again for any purpose—that you cannot have truck with False Idols;
- the person (probably American) who devised False Alligator was chastised by the Lord, and, lo, the Lord did smite him down, and others like him.

If you have any spare time in Rome, you can also buy him some shirts, as long as you don't allow him to pick them out himself. Or, *forse,* a nice, buttery-leather wallet. It is so sensual. In fact, many modern Italian men fondle their wallets in lieu of sex.

LONDON

London is a man's city. It is the color of a man's suit. It doesn't have a lot of daffy cupolas and things, and the people don't use a lot of queer words that have accent marks over them, and a man can almost certainly get himself a drink that isn't pink or green, or named after a Catholic saint.

It is a good compromise city for the two of you to go to. You can split up during the day, and *you* can watch all those puffy, colorful British ceremonies that sadly herald the Last Breaths of a Dying Empire, while *he* can hole up in a pub somewhere, watch jolly, jowly guys play darts, and discover that even in London, as in the rest of Europe, there are nudes in the daily newspaper.

DESTINATION: THE TROPICS

It is a well-known fact that Bogart fell for Lauren Bacall while filming *To Have and Have Not* in the Caribbean; and

STEPHANIE BRUSH

Ingrid Bergman and Roberto Rossellini romanced on the volcanic island of Stromboli. For this reason, you should make sure that your man sees a lot of movies. A lot of men don't know that unless they can burst through a length of mosquito netting with one swipe of a machete, and suck adder poisoning out of your leg, while balancing a tray of margaritas, then you can hardly be expected to keep romance on the brain.

Yet the tropics can pose a lot of problems for couples on romantic vacations. Most forward-thinking Caribbean airlines now put the following information on your ticket, in order to ease confusion:

- The destination to which they are sending you.
- The destination to which they are sending your luggage.

But none of this really helps in the long run. Your contraceptives will be *in* your luggage.

You will not realize it until it is too late. You will experiment with using guava paste, Bain de Soleil, and Crest as spermicides.

You will find them to be ineffective.

DESTINATION: MEXICAN PYRAMIDS

It is always a bad idea to take a man to Mayan ruins.

He always says, "I can walk up that pyramid, honey," and you say, "No, you can't," but he will, anyway, and afterward he will be no good for sex for weeks.

The Mayan civilization died out because after the Mayan pyramids were built, all the men wanted to walk up them; and then afterward they were no good for sex for weeks.

SEPARATE VACATIONS

I do not advise taking separate vacations because it is passing up a valuable opportunity for Learning.

Traveling with a man, you are bound to make at least one Important Discovery. Sometimes it's that you are living with a total stranger. Or, sometimes, it's that *he's* living with a total stranger. But you would not find these things out if the two of you just sat home all the time.

If you can get through a night in a miserable *pension* behind a goat tannery in Barcelona without lots of unpleasantness and mutual recrimination, then your relationship is in good shape.

And bear this in mind: A woman who takes a vacation alone in order to "find herself" usually ends up in one place. In the shower stall in cabin one at the Bates Motel.

I probably mean this metaphorically.

EPILOGUE

Some Parting Words to Live By

IF you have read this far, you may still be asking yourself, "Does this mean that *I* can now resolve the pressing man issues in *my* life? Do I possess the proper tools now? Do I have the smarts, eh?" Or even, "Do people who write *books* have the right to tell me how to resolve the pressing man issues in my life?"

Verily, there is a thirst for knowledge in America. What does the future hold vis-à-vis men, and what new frontiers are being explored?

As a result of their fear and confusion on this subject, many women have adopted an indifferent, callous object-oriented attitude. They insist that the mood enhancement formerly supplied by men in their lives can now be achieved through the installation of ion machines, and even stationary bicycles. (They feel that their oxygenated blood will cause them to manufacture thrilling chemicals that will put men out of their minds permanently and forever.)

But many women have not given up entirely and feel that they want to Give Pair Bonding a Go. They've demonstrated their faith in men; they've already sunk a large amount of capital into issues like training and remedial work; and they feel that the investment can, and, indeed, should, pay off.

What these women need is a small, daily shot in the arm. Maybe just some words of advice that they can carry around in their wallets (much like old, yellowed ANN LANDERS columns) to repeat in times of need.

Here are some Words, and I hope they serve you well:

1. DO NOT THINK ABOUT TRYING TO MAKE IT THROUGH A LIFETIME WITH A MAN. JUST CONCENTRATE ON MAKING IT THROUGH A YEAR.

STATISTICS say that if you can make it through the first twelve months, you are in terrific shape. You will know his significant habits and his internal rhythms, and what foods he refuses to eat before nine in the morning, and, *most important,* HE will have gotten used to YOU. Men will never admit this, but order, and, yes, routine are essential elements in their personal cosmos: THE REASON A MAN WILL NOT TRY TO SPLIT UP WITH YOU AFTER A YEAR OR SO IS HIS LIMITLESS FEAR OF BREAKING IN A NEW MODEL.

A man fears that he will get stuck with a new girlfriend who is "creative" in the A.M., who may say things like, "About breakfast, honey . . . *I've* got an idea!" (*You,* you see, have been with him long enough to know that breakfast IS NOT THE SORT OF MEAL ONE SHOULD GET "IDEAS" ABOUT. It is the same as betraying his trust. And trust is everything.)

2. MEN REALLY ARE SUPERIOR TO WOMEN IN MANY WAYS

MANY women have tried to argue this point in recent years, but it happens to be true.

- Men can throw a discus or a hardball or a large rock farther than women can. Society has benefited incalculably from these skills, as I don't have to tell you.
- Men will always get better tables for business lunches than women will, even three hundred years from now.
- Men look better in brown than women do.
- Men are better card players than women, since they often include entertaining SOUND EFFECTS at crucial moments.
- Men look good in suspenders, whereas all women look ridiculous in suspenders; especially Olivia Newton-John.
- Men do not suffer from premenstrual syndrome (PMS), and do not change moods if they do not feel like changing moods.
- Men are important to have around in an emergency. They have very strong index fingers, and can dial a telephone very quickly.
- Men will always have superior buttocks to women; even if they never exercise and eat potato chips many times a week. (In fact, the longer you live with a man, the smaller and firmer his buttocks get, and the larger yours get. It is possible that some sort of *cellular transfer* takes place over time, as the two of you sleep together.)

And yet despite all these amazing and true facts, no one knows why it is that men are unable to wrap birthday packages without complaining and making a big mess and asking you to do it for them.

3. MEN WANT LOVE AND ACCEPTANCE JUST AS MUCH AS WOMEN DO

YES, it is hard to believe this sometimes, when the greatest compliment a man can muster is that you're a vast improvement over the years he spent in the dark watching midget wrestling on VHF.

But it's true.

Maybe there've been times when you thought that just about *anything* would be preferable to your man. You've caught yourself estimating what his trade-in worth would be in a recession year; you've considered leaving him on a street corner with a little note pinned to his collar saying, "Please . . . ANYONE."

But you must accept in the end that men are one of our great natural resources, sure to appreciate in value over the years to come.

More and more, you can take them just about anywhere and not be embarrassed. In a harsh, uncompromising world, this is nothing to sneeze at.

Acknowledgments

There are many people who have helped make this book possible. The English Department of Pleasantville High School, Pleasantville, New York; the makers of Martinson coffee and Executive Ko-Rec-Type; the fine gentlemen at Mariella Pizza, Third Avenue, New York City; my doorman Vinny. Also, my good friends Wanda Di Benedetto and Danny Pelavin. And Anne Porter for helping me keep up my stamina, and Daun Paris Hauspurg for having limitless faith for the last ten years.

Most especially, I thank my publisher, Joni Evans, my agent, Richard Pine, and my wonderful editor, Marjorie Williams.

And I thank all the men I have ever known.

About the Author

Stephanie Brush is a native of Cleveland, Ohio. She has written for *Viva, Self, Signature,* and *Cosmopolitan* magazines, and traveled throughout the known world researching this book. She lives in Greenwich Village, has no pets, and enjoys television.